CELTIC THREADS

Exploring the Wisdom of Our Heritage

Padraigín Clancy

VERITAS

First published 1999 by
Veritas Publications
7/8 Lower Abbey Street
Dublin 1

Copyright © The individual contributors 1999

ISBN 1 85390 499 6

British Library Cataloguing
in Publication Data.
A catalogue record for
this book is available
from the British Library.

Cover design by Bill Bolger
The front cover photograph of Corp Naomh Bell Shrine (from
Templecross, County Westmeath, ca. tenth to fifteenth
century) is reproduced by permission of the National Museum
of Ireland. Background detail is from Newgrange, Slane,
County Meath, ca. 2000 BC.
Printed in the Republic of Ireland by Betaprint Ltd, Dublin

TO IRELAND IN THE COMING TIMES

–W. B. Yeats

CONTENTS

INTRODUCTION

Ireland in the late twentieth century is seeing a new turning towards matters 'Celtic'. In fact, fasten the word on to anything nowadays and it will surely sell. It is being liberally applied to describe everything, from the mundanity of 'Celtic Laundries' to the sublimity of the 'Celtic Soul'. Its ambit includes our economy: the Celtic Tiger; our music: Celtic Rock; Celtic Perfume; Celtic Helicopters; Celtic Birds; Celtic Chocolates – you name it we have it, and it is Celtic!

What is happening? It is interesting to note that much of what passes for Celtic is quite simply Irish, yet the latter term is not being used. Why not? Are we re-identifying ourselves as Irish people in the late twentieth century under the banner of Celtic? Is it that the word has a broader appeal than 'Irish' and suggests a community that is more 'outward rather than inward' looking, inclusive rather than insular?

There is also a hint of the mysterious in the 'Celtic'. As we move towards a greater assimilation with Europe, perhaps we are seeking to return to that which makes us special, which has somehow not been entirely colonised – neither Anglicised, Roman Catholicised, Americanised, nor Europeanised. Something that allows us to reside on the periphery with confidence, that might even have Europe and the wider world turning towards *us*.

Whatever its genesis, part of what is happening is an embracing of what is being termed 'Celtic spirituality'. This book is a collection of essays on that subject. It seeks to represent what is happening in the field of Celtic spirituality in Ireland in the twilight years of the twentieth century. Each author is at the forefront of the field – drawing on the Celtic spiritual tradition as a central inspiration in their work.

The contributors hail from Ulster, Munster, Leinster and Connaught and include a female politician and member of the European parliament, a Benedictine monk, a Methodist minister, a noted female singer, a Jesuit priest, a feminist theologian, a psycho-therapist, an Irish folklorist, a philosopher-gardener, a Celtic priest, a Church of Ireland clergyman, a stress-management counsellor, a Redemptorist missionary, a Brigidine sister, a native Irish speaker and a returned exile.

In many respects the line-up represents the journey that Irish/Celtic spirituality has made in the twentieth century, from octogenarian Diarmuid Ó Laoghaire SJ, who ploughed a lonely furrow during the early and mid-decades of this century, through to someone such as myself; a child of the sixties, a layperson and woman, committed to the practice and teaching of the Christian heritage through the Irish/Celtic culture – a ministry which as yet holds no definable role in the Church to which I belong, the Roman Catholic Church.

Each author has been invited to contribute from their specific area of interest. Reflecting their various disciplines, some have taken an academic approach and simply describe an element of the Celtic tradition, while others have drawn on their personal story and experience, working in spiritual direction with individuals and groups countrywide. Entitled *Celtic Threads*, each essay is simply that: a thread in the spiritual wisdom of our heritage.

Drawing from the pre-Christian and Christian 'Celtic' story, the collection moves through the wonders and the darknesses of the Celtic tradition. It asks: Is Celtic spirituality soul-food or junk-food? How can it be of value today? Why is the archetype of war predominant in the Irish psyche? What about the quality of mercy? How can Celtic spirituality contribute to a process for peace?

The essays explore the lives of the early Irish saints: why was the practice of exile/pilgrimage of such importance to them? Who is Colm Cille? What about Brigit – why is there a return to *her-story*? How can the legacy of Celtic prayer, song and folk tradition enrich our liturgy and worship? What can modern Irish society relearn through the typically Celtic values of hospitality and respect for the divine immanent in creation? What projects are happening nowadays in places of ancient sanctity such as Glendalough and Kildare?

That there is a real thirst for a return to the well of our native wisdom is clear. The work of these authors and the recent resounding success of John O'Donohue's *Anam Chara* has something to teach us. Perhaps the answer to our return to the Celtic lies ultimately in the spiritual search. Amidst the freneticism of modern Irish life we might ask ourselves: what is happening to the Life of the Spirit? Will the Celtic Tiger be constrained or are we in danger of allowing it prey on the Celtic Soul? How can our increased economic confidence lend itself creatively to the realisation of a more life-giving society for each person on the island?

Sometimes when I gaze at the Ardagh Chalice or peer into the extraordinary genius of the Book of Kells or scramble around in the ruins of the once-great Aran and Clonmacnoise, I reflect that we are a broken people, humanly and culturally. Just as the emigrant's grandchild is compelled to return to the old home-place for healing and inspiration, perhaps we now need to return and remember – to make our selves more whole or *holy*. As we look to the future, Celtic spirituality may offer us a certain refuge that is not only revitalising but necessary.

In the end, there is no final tapestry – threads are all we possess; what we do with them is up to us collectively. Our first obligation may be to weave a harness for the Celtic Tiger, nurture the Celtic Soul, and with determination create a more compassionate, just, honest and equal society. If we want a better Ireland, a better Europe and World, can we dare to go forward, without minding the Life of the Spirit, individual and communal, into the twenty-first century!

Solas Chríost inár measc...

Padraigín Clancy
15 Lúnasa/August 1999

THE UNCREATED CONSCIENCE
OF OUR RACE

Mary T. Condren

I remember it clearly. Home for a visit from the United States, I travelled to Newgrange with my mother and three-year-old niece. Mid-summer, and the weather was cold and wet. The single tour-guide trekked us through the fields and we stood, all four of us, in the chamber, while she recounted the then-dominant interpretations of Newgrange. For ten pence I purchased the only available photocopied *interpretation* and home we went, cold, wet – and miserable!

Twenty years later and here I am back at Newgrange, with its shuttle-buses, extensive car-park, suited guides, bookshop, restaurant, and fine new interpretative centre. Bookings are in place for months ahead. The waiting list for viewing the winter solstice is now closed. No tour of Ireland is complete without a visit. Celtic spirituality has arrived. Why do I feel like running?

Celtic Spirituality: Soul-Food or Junk-Food?

Back in 1976, as editor of *Movement,* the journal of the Student Christian Movement of Britain and Ireland, I published a special issue: *Celtic Theology: An Introduction.* My hope was that by revisiting the old Celtic sources we might find the basis for a Celtic liberation theology. Surely, we asked, in the old Celtic sources there was hope, vision, imagination, soul-food for those of us disenchanted by the Roman or British appropriations of the Christian traditions in the interests of their various colonial enterprises.

Now, one can't go into a bookshop in Ireland without being confronted (assaulted?) by Celtic spirituality. Beautifully packaged, complete with triple spirals, Celtic crosses, shots of

1

Newgrange, the books draw liberally on Celtic poetry, music, and utterly sanitised versions of the 'Lives' of saints. Has Celtic spirituality become a product, a commodity, a neat easy-to-assemble, do-it-yourself package of consumer goodies? No longer soul-food – more like junk-food for the mind-numbing culture of the late twentieth century? Have profits replaced prophets? Has spiritual dessert replaced the spirituality of the desert?

I ask these questions as we draw toward the close of the second millennium. With the meteoric rise of computer and satellite technology, television and video games, we are saturated with imagery, hungry for excitement, bombarded by advertising, seduced by the promises of advanced capitalism. Not the life hereafter but the good life here and now is what counts. Every desire can be felt, expressed and met, providing we bow down and adore the gods who have made it all possible, at least in the West: the One-Third World.

For the billions of people living in the Two-Thirds World – China, India, Africa – our old colonial outposts, the story is radically different. Diseases, famine, malnourishment, war, with weapons supplied by the One-Third World, are all pervasive. These countries, economically crippled, spend more on repaying their debts to the One-Third World than they do on education, medicine or housing.

How quickly, how easily, we forget our own recent poverty and famines. Now the darlings of Europe (and still with our hands in the till), we dare not speak too loudly of the legacy of colonial intrusion and exploitation lest the fleshpots of Europe and its allies be snatched from our grasp. For the spiritual fast-food generations, Celtic gurus and heroes bring certainty, not questions – Angel Dust – short-term quick fixes and long-term spiritual, ecological and political death.

What Has Happened to the Land of Saints and Scholars?

Thomas Cahill once wrote a book entitled *How the Irish Saved Civilisation*. His research drew on the contributions made by Irish missionaries to Europe during the Dark Ages. While we might be mildly amused by Cahill's title, the question remains: Do we now have anything to offer, or is Celtic spirituality destined to become simply an instrument of pacification, or a comfort for the bewildered?

What has happened to the Land of Saints and Scholars? Where are the ideals espoused by the spiritual leaders of the Celtic past? What do they have to offer to our civilisation today, a civilisation beset with terrorism and genocide, where war and the threat of war have become the dominant grammar of human political relations? I believe that we have something to offer and my assertion derives from continuing to reflect on the prophetic injunction: 'I desire mercy, not sacrifice' (Hosea 6:1-6; Matthew 9:13, 12:1-8).

'I Desire Mercy, Not Sacrifice'

Of all the biblical aphorisms that have passed into the parlance of Western culture, this is surely the one most ignored. It is ignored for precisely the same reasons that explain why Europe and the West have become the world powers they are. My basic thesis is this: that sacrifice, not mercy, has become the dominant religion of the West, giving rise to liturgies, rituals, theologies, spiritualities and political practices in which our very identities are sacrificially achieved at someone else's expense.

The images of the Christ, who died for all 'in the sacrifice to end all sacrifices', are replaced by the Tomb of the Unknown Soldier who gave his life for all, 'in the war to end all wars'. The language, imagery and propaganda of sacrifice and war merge inexorably in the twentieth century – a lethal combination – and never more so than in Ireland itself where, especially in

Northern Ireland, the old Reformation debates about sacrifice are played out to their logical and lethal conclusions.

Sacrifice/War and the Creation of 'Otherness'

In this short article it would be impossible to do justice to the question of sacrifice – its definition, workings, or systems of interpretation. I will concentrate simply on one issue: the radical *otherness* induced by sacrificial practices. By this I mean the way in which sacrifice apparently enables us to enter into a new world beyond the routine everyday world. This new world becomes *sacred, holy*, or otherwise worthy of veneration.

Sacrificial practices bring about this world by the voluntary or involuntary killing of the sacrificial victim or its surrogates. Religions are brought into being or renewed by the sacrifices of their founders. New political regimes are brought into being by the sacrifices of war. Those who have died establish a *sacred debt* to be paid by their descendants.

In the current Northern Irish context, it is a commonplace for those who wish to continue the struggle to say things such as: 'this is not the Ireland my (father, brother, forebears) died for.' Such sacred debts as those established in sacrifice/war lead to a perpetual cycle of violence and/or revenge. For this cycle of violence to continue and for this *sacrality* to be maintained there needs to be perpetual opposition. When the old enemies are defeated, new enemies are created. Indeed, war is *the* metaphor for religions founded on sacrifice: wars against the flesh, the Devil, the unconverted, the infidels – anyone who threatens my precariously established identity. Participation in sacrifice enables one to live on the high moral ground, an indispensable corollary of war.

Sacrifice and the Celtic Otherworld

What has this to do with Celtic spirituality? Just about everything. The Old Irish never relinquished the sense of the

4

Otherworld. Celtic consciousness thrived on breaking down the barriers between life and death, poetry and reason, symbol and sign, womb and tomb, the unconscious and the conscious. But if these worlds were held together tenaciously, at times of sacrifice they were split apart and the sacrificially created oppositions reigned supreme. The humility, awe, reverence and holy fear experienced in the face of the Otherworld was ultimately transformed into pride, arrogance and the urge to dominate the Other. A people who once might have prospered and thrived living on the edge of Otherness, we now persecute and reject the Other in ourselves. More alarmingly, we persecute the Others all around us – anyone who threatens our precariously established identity.

Fairies were once symbols of playful unpredictability. Attached to homosexuals, the word 'fairies' is now derisory. Far from holding the boundaries between this world and another world, between this sex and another sex, fairies have become figures of ridicule and even hate.

Blackness traditionally symbolises our negativity, those unresolved feelings of envy, murder or hate that all of us have but largely keep under control. Attached to people of colour, our negativity is displaced onto Others who act as our scapegoats, allowing us to wallow in our own self-righteousness.

If sacrificially achieved certainties are at the heart of the problem, where should we look for an alternative? Given the torrid history, especially of this century, how can we begin to explore new ways of *being* in the new millennium? Perhaps we could look again at the words 'I desire mercy, not sacrifice'.

Mercy and the Quest for the 'World of the Other'

The quest for the Otherworld might seem difficult for a post-modern generation, but perhaps the metaphor should be replaced by the quest for the World of the Other – arguably, a quest that has a great deal more in common with the message and spirit of the Gospels.

Could this be the question of mercy? The radical turning to the Other when the Other is faced with stoning, persecution, victimisation, scapegoating and enforced exile? How is mercy cultivated? What are its practices?

Not surprisingly, since St Brigit of Ireland (ca AD 500), among others, took the Beatitude *mercy*, this question must have been a concern for our Celtic ancestors, and the sources suggest several approaches. Within the limits here we will only have room to look at one: the practice of pilgrimage or exile.

The Practice of Exile/Pilgrimage in the Celtic Christian Tradition

Irish society at the time of the introduction of Christianity was essentially tribal and often matri-focal (revolving around the mother). Loyalty to kin was paramount. One could not fight one's brother or one's kin within several degrees of relationship – all traced back to the mother.

The problem here was that excessive familiarity with one's family, tribe or country often led to forms of nepotism or inherited privilege, which allow little growth in the social structure or room for excellence achieved through other means. Whereas today we have developed a highly abstract system of justice, in those days justice was restorative and restitutive and applied largely only to those within one's system of kinship obligations. Inter-tribal warfare and cattle-raiding were the norm, leading to lives that were often nasty, brutish and short.

Celtic mythology for its part, and certainly in the time of the patriarchal Celts, was largely heroic. Death-defying feats signalled out the hero, and the wiser Celtic monks knew there might be little difference between the warrior and religious heroes. How could Celtic Christianity make a difference?

To begin with, they addressed the question of martyrdom – so often the defining feature of early Christianity. They asked:

> Now there are three kinds of martyrdom which are counted as a cross to man, that is to say, white martyrdom, and green martyrdom and red martyrdom. This is the white martyrdom to man when he separates for the sake of God from everything he loves, although he suffers fasting or labour thereat. This is the green martyrdom to him, when by means of fasting or labour he separates him from his desires, or suffers toil in penance and repentance. This is the red martyrdom to him, endurance of a cross or destruction for Christ's sake, as has happened to the apostles in the persecution of the wicked and in teaching the law of God. These three kinds of martyrdom are comprised in the carnal ones who resort to good repentance, who separate from their desires, who pour forth their blood in fasting and in labour for Christ's sake. (Cambrai Homily)[1]

White martyrdom was one of the main impetuses behind the *peregrinatio pro/Christi* movement, which helped spread Christianity in Europe by non-violent means. Many Irish sailed off in boats without oars, trusting in the mercy of God and abandoning themselves to the will of God as to where they might land. In the *Life of Columcille* the saint gives the theological reason underlying this movement as that of emulating Abraham, who left his homeland in response to the word of God:

> It is the parting of soul and body for a man to leave his kindred and his country and go from them to strange distant lands, in exile and perpetual pilgrimage.[2]

To separate from one's kin, or to separate from one's desires are equally valid means of expressing commitment, comparable to red martyrdom. In other words, these early spiritual leaders were trying to find ways of enabling soul-searchers to separate from the familiarity of their kin, the comforts of home, their addiction to desires. For the Irish, the breaking of kin relationships was probably the most excruciating part of this spiritual exercise. To die in exile with a stranger soil for grave was, for the Irish, the extreme of abnegation and the crown of religious life.[3]

Exile/Pilgrimage and the Cultivation of Mercy

As those who go into exile can attest, estrangement from one's origins can serve spiritual growth and the cultivation of spiritual self-reliance, together with an enhanced awareness of one's vulnerability, transience and utter dependence. Pilgrimage into the natural wilds cultivates our sense of awe, reverence, and gratitude for the mysteries of creation – a gratitude that carries with it profound awareness of our ecological responsibility.[4]

Is it possible for someone immersed in the majesty of the sea to contemplate dumping nuclear waste? Can someone who has embraced a tree or stood under its shade, or watched it change with the seasons, blithely contemplate tearing it down to make way for more and more cars?

Some of the earliest monastic settlements were by the edge of the sea, near cliffs, where the full majesty of nature exploded, illuminated, and rested, paraphrasing the rhythms of our natural life itself, with all its vicissitudes. When we are in touch with our own vulnerability, we empathise with the vulnerability of others, as the following early legend attests:

Mael Anfaidh, Abbot of Darindse.... It is this Mael Anfaidh who saw one day a little bird weeping and making plaint. 'O my God', he said, 'what has happened there? I vow that I will not eat food until it is made known to me.' While he was there, he saw an angel coming towards him. 'Good, there, cleric', said the angel, 'let it not cause you any more worry. Molua son of Ocha has died, and this is why the living things bewail him, because he never killed a living thing, whether big or small, and the animals no less than men lament him, and the little bird you see'.[5]

Contemporary Irish Exiles: Joyce and Beckett

The early monastic leaders embraced exile and pilgrimage for much the same reasons as contemporary Irish writers such as James Joyce and Samuel Beckett embraced it: for the sake of their souls. Contemporary feminist scholars, such as Julia Kristeva, Luce Irigaray and Helene Cixous, appalled at the resurgence of retrograde nationalisms, the exploitation of migrant workers, the treatment of women and the wars of ethnic cleansing, similarly advocate the philosophy and practice of exile. In exile, in isolation, we are brought up sharp against our own strangeness and mystery, enabling us to embrace the strangers among us, to appreciate diversity rather than persecuting it in ourselves or in others.

Yet everything, including exile or pilgrimage, can be turned into yet another fetish or false security. Religious pilgrimages, where everything is predictable, ritualised and comfortable, can be equally corrupting. As Brigit is reputed to have told her resident bishop, Conleth, when he set out for Rome in search of fine vestments:

> To come to Rome, to come to Rome,
> Much of trouble, little of profit.
> The thing thou seekest here

If thou bring not with thee, thou findest not.
Great folly, great madness,
Great ruin, great insanity,
Since thou has set out for death
That thou should be in disobedience to the Son of Mary.[6]

Making Us Think

In conclusion, one could do worse than reflect on a story told of one of our Irish exiles, Johannes Scotus Eriugena. An Irish monk, he travelled across Europe. At the end of one of his lectures he was attacked and fatally stabbed by a knife-wielding student. Asked to account for his actions, the student is said to have simply replied: 'He made us think.'[7]

Pilgrimages or exiles that do not make us think, far from being challenging, can lock us into our old versions of truth. They close our ears to the cries of Others, keeping out the strangers or precariously established identities. They can feed our addiction to answers, blocking out the very questions that might need to be asked.

At the end of the twentieth century, Celtic spirituality worthy of the name must return to the question of *mercy*. Minds that are stuffed and stifled with easy answers must learn to ask new questions; identities that are sacrificially achieved at someone else's expense must be radically unsettled; spirits that are dead must be raised to new life: through the redemptive power of forging in the smithy of the soul, the uncreated conscience of our race.

> April 26. Mother is putting my second hand clothes in order. She prays, now she says, that I may learn in my own life and away from home and friends what the heart is and what it feels. So be it. Welcome, O Life! I go to encounter for the millionth time the reality of experience

and to forge in the smithy of my soul the uncreated conscience of my race.

April 27. Old father, old artificer, stand me now and ever in good stead.[8]

CELTIC SPIRITUALITY: A HOLY EMBRACE OF SPIRIT AND NATURE

Dolores Whelan

Perhaps the word 'Celtic' does not adequately describe the spiritual tradition that I am attempting to articulate, because that would limit this spiritual tradition to only one of the many influences that has shaped its evolution. Perhaps, too, that word is in such a state of overuse that one is not at all sure what is meant by it. It does seem, however, that the use of 'Celtic' allows us to conjure up something that existed in a space and time different and distant from the present and that there is a realisation that what existed then, holds some elements that are both missing and needed by us as we travel on our soul's journey today.

W. B. Yeats wrote, 'The history of the world is a stream of souls not a catalogue of facts'.[1] I suggest that it might be important to trace some threads in the soul or spiritual journey of this country and its people.

Arrival of the Celts in Ireland

The Celts arrived in Ireland around AD 500 and it is thought that when they arrived they encountered here an already spiritual people who had their own religious practices and rites. According to mythologist T. W. Rolleston, the Celts were a spiritually sensitive people, who did not overthrow the beliefs and rituals of the indigenous people, but rather honoured them and gradually absorbed them into their own culture. This cross-cultural event seemed to be a two-way process, allowing a symbiosis of old and new. Rolleston writes:

What is quite clear is that when the Celts got to western Europe they found there a people with a powerful priesthood, ritual, and imposing religious monuments. The inference, as I read the facts, seems to be that Druidism in its essential features was imposed upon the imaginative and sensitive nature of the Celts by the earlier population of Western Europe; the Megalithic people.[2]

This symbiosis resulted in the strengthening of religious practices and in the revamping and restoration of the sacred sites of the megalithic peoples by the Celts.

Coming of Christianity

When Christianity arrived in Ireland, probably in the first or second century AD, it took root in a very specific way. In a similar manner to what had happened when the Celts arrived, it would seem that there was, once again, a cross-cultural mingling of ideologies and ritual practices. The unique form of Christianity that emerged, due to the particular ambience into which the Christian message became embedded, is nowadays often referred to as Celtic Christianity.

So what was the ambience that Christianity, already influenced by Greek, Roman and Jewish culture, encountered when it arrived in Ireland? Evidence suggests that there was a belief among these early peoples that God was fully present in the created, material world. The elements of the natural world, for example, were seen as a medium through which the glory of God shone. This is later reflected in the Celtic Christian tradition, as the following prayer attributed to St Patrick and given in translation here indicates:

I arise today
Through the strength of heaven:

Light of sun,
Radiance of moon,
Splendour of fire,
Speed of lightning,
Swiftness of wind,
Depth of sea,
Stability of earth,
Firmness of rock.[3]

The Immanent, Dynamic and Creative Aspects of God

The theme of the immanence of God figures strongly at this time of transition. A seventh-century poem tells of how the pre-Christian, mythological Ethne Alba asked St Patrick about the new Christian God by reference to the God of her own knowing:

Who is God and where is His dwelling?
Is He ever living?

Is He in heaven,
or on the earth?
In the seas,
in the rivers,
in the mountains,
in the valleys?[4]

The response attributed to Patrick emphasises the theme of divine immanence:

Our God, God of all men [people],
God of heaven and earth, seas and rivers,
God of sun and moon, of all the stars,
God of high mountains and lowly valleys,
God over heaven, and in heaven and under heaven.[5]

Elsewhere in this response, Patrick refers to the dynamic and creative aspects of God:

> He inspires all things,
> He quickens all things
> He is over all things,
> He supports all things.

> He makes the light of the sun to shine,
> He surrounds the moon and the stars,
> and He has made wells in the arid earth,
> placed dry islands in the sea
> and stars for the service
> of the greater luminaries.[6]

This passage indicates a divinity present in the world, eternally co-creating, and certainly not an austere God in the sky, with high empty space between God and his creation. We see reflected a central aspect of Celtic Christianity; the holy embrace of nature and spirit, a sense of holy intimacy between humanity, the natural world and divinity. Here we experience what H. J. Massingham describes as:

> a gleam of the new philosophy of heaven and earth in interdependence and interaction, formulated by a culture in vital contact with its ancient nature worship.[7]

There was also a recognition that we humans share the world, not only with the animals and plants but also with other realms unseen, yet knowable – an awareness of the existence of many worlds and dimensions in the universe, not all of them accessible to the human senses. This was a mind-set that held an appreciation of the hidden, transcendent and immanent aspects of the divine and which was later echoed by Meister

Eckhart when he wrote 'outside God there is nothing but nothing'.[8]

Justice and Right Relationship

For the Celtic and other peoples, including the Jewish people, the concept of justice was connected, not to abstract legal ideologies, but to the concept of right relationship. For the early Celtic Christian, loving God required living in harmony with nature. They took seriously the injunction in Deuteronomy: 'those who love God will have plentiful crops and good pasture for their cattle'.

This scripture echoed the ancient pre-Christian Irish tradition of the *Bainis Rí* – the sacred marriage of a king with the goddess of the land. This wedding, which took place before a king commenced his rule, was symbolic of the world of the humans, the natural world and the unseen worlds coming together in an interdependent union. If the rule of a king was just, then the goddess of the land (Ireland) gave forth in abundance. If the king did not act and rule justly, then the land withheld its bounty; the king was then seen as unsuccessful and unfit to remain in office.

The love of God was therefore translated into practical terms by taking care of all of God's creation. The opposite of love, for these people, was not hate, but greed, which arises from a lack of reverence for creation and a lack of knowledge of one's place in the greater scheme of things. This relationship, therefore, was not sentimental. It understood both the strength and the paradoxical fragility of the natural world.

Celtic Saints: Stories of Right Relationship

Several stories from early Christian times tell of how the harmony with nature could be disrupted when people became selfish and broke the bonds of right relationship. One such story tells of how this led to the produce of the earth being too weak to support people.

> All the saints came to Columba's Durrow to fast against God. They were furious with the Almighty because the penitents whom they had put on bread and water to make reparation for their sins had all died. An angel came to rebuke the saints for their anger at what seemed to be a divine injustice. 'Wonder not if the bread and water cannot sustain the penitents today', said the heavenly messenger, 'the fruits and the plants of the earth have been devastated so that there is neither strength and force in them to support anyone. The falsehood and the sins of men have robbed the earth with its fruits of their strength and force. When men were obedient to God's will the plants of the earth retained their proper strengths'.[9]

Another story tells us of the horror of a saint at the overuse of food and the consequential waste of resources. The story is about a saint named Neot who lived in Celtic Britain.

> This holy man had a pool by his settlement in which three fish swam. Every day he ate one fish and every morning there were three fish still swimming in the pool. One day the saint fell sick and did not feel like eating anything at all. Still the three fishes went on swimming in the pool. Eventually Neot's companions, hoping to tempt the saint to eat by offering a choice of dishes, cooked each fish in a different manner. When the saint saw what food was spread before him he was aghast. Immediately he recovered sufficiently to order the three untouched dishes to be emptied into the water. At once the fish returned to life and swam away. Now restored to

health, Neot went back to his practice of eating one of the inexhaustible supply each day.[10]

This story speaks of the need to use resources wisely so that sustainability is ensured. It hints at the saint's understanding that abundance in life is linked with an appropriate use of resources, including gratitude for food and a reverence for its source. This understanding of abundance is strikingly different from the present notion of abundance, which is seen as endless consumerism.

Other stories from the early Celtic Christian period tell of the intimate and mutual relationship of the saints and animals. One such story tells of how sea-otters dried St Cuthbert after he had spent the night praying and chanting in the sea, and also of how a horse found food beneath a thatched roof for him.

When St Columba was dying, it was his horse that first knew about it and began the mourning process. Many stories tell about the saints being lead to the site of their settlement by an animal, such as St Ciaran of Clonmacnoise being lead by a stag to his hermitage on the shores of Lough Ree.

'An Eye Washed Miraculously Clear'

The early Christian believers and saints were reputed to have great healing powers. This power was often connected with their keen knowledge of the healing qualities of plants and herbs, which they probably inherited from the Druids. They were also thought to have inherited the gifts of clairvoyance and psychic power. Their relationship with the animal and plant world was finely tuned and developed through intensive spiritual practice. Robin Flower describes it as follows:

> It was because they brought into that environment an eye washed miraculously clear by continuous spiritual

exercise, that they first in Europe had that strange vision of natural things in an almost unnatural purity.[11]

Flower is referring to the capacity to see into and beyond the physicality of a thing, to see its non-material, essential quality – its spiritual essence. It is to have the eye and the mind-set to see 'the sun behind the sun' or 'the mountain behind the mountain'. This concept is expressed many times throughout different historical eras in writings from the Celtic tradition. It frequently occurs in the poetry of Patrick Kavanagh, a twentieth-century Irish mystical poet, who cannot imagine a little piece of Monaghan (his home place) that cannot also be a piece of Eden.

Here we experience again the key belief of the Celtic and pre-Celtic people: that the spiritual world infuses the material world, and that the material world emerges from the spiritual, non-material world. Also, that there is an unbroken wholeness in the worlds we inhabit, and that by 'seeing' the spiritual world shining through the material world, we can understand and experience that unbroken wholeness of the universe, which mystics of all spiritual traditions aspire to and speak about.

Muthos and Logos

This facility for 'seeing' was greatly enhanced by the fact that the Celtic Christian world was one that was inhabited by the world of *muthos* or myth, as well as *logos* or the rational world.

The world of myth allows us to soften the edge of our perception, to loosen the rigidity of boundaries that separate the material and the non-material. It allows us to develop our imagination to see with the soft focus of inner eyes, to hear with inner ears, to sense images that are gossamer thin and would not survive in the harsh world of logos. These are images and worlds that come alive and flourish in the dim lights of candles and firesides.

The Celtic Christian mind-set, for example, was at home with stories about angels and spirits from the New Testament. This was due to their highly developed inner worlds and skills of imagination, which allowed them to enter at will the non-material, yet real world where angels and spirits reside. These highly developed skills of imagination were used as a faculty of perception, expressing what was inside and outside the mind of a person who was deeply attuned to the inner world. A beautiful example of this comes from the *Carmina Gadelica*. Alexander Carmichael records Barbara MacPhee's experience of seeing the sun dance on an Easter Sunday morning. The extract from Barbara is given in translation from the Gallic:

> The people say that the sun dances on this day in joy for a risen Saviour. Old Barbara MacPhee at Dreimsdale saw this once, but only once, during her long life. And the good woman, of high natural intelligence, described in poetic language and with religious fervor what she saw or believed she saw from the summit of Benmore.

> 'The glorious gold-bright sun was after
> rising on the crests of the great hills, and it
> was changing colour – green, purple, red
> blood-red, white, intense-white, and gold-white
> like the glory of the God of the elements
> to the children of men. It was dancing up and down
> in exultation at the joyous resurrection of the beloved
> Saviour of victory.

> To be thus privileged, a person must
> ascend to the top of the highest hill before
> sunrise, and believe that the God who
> makes the small blade of grass to grow is

the same God who makes the large, massive sun to move.'[12]

The Legacy of Folk Tradition

The *Carmina Gadelica*, the writings of Douglas Hyde and much of the works collected from rural Irish spiritual traditions in the nineteenth century give a wonderful account of how early Celtic Christianity was preserved in a relatively pure and pristine way in places such as the islands and highlands of Scotland, most parts of Ireland and West Wales.

Through these writings we get to glimpse into the world, the lives and the mind-set of the people who lived in these places and whose spirituality is recorded in prayer, blessing and invocation. These prayers allow us to sense the fabric and colour of the landscape in which they lived, loved, fought, gave birth and died. They reflect for us an egalitarian spirituality, belonging to and owned by the people in their daily lives. God is not distant but engaged intimately in the lives of the people.

The following examples, once again from *Carmina Gadelica*, give an acute flavour of this:

Blessing of Journey
O God bless every step
that I am taking,
and bless the ground
beneath my feet.

Consecration of the Seed
I will go out to sow the seed,
In the name of him who gave it growth.

Blessing of the Kindling of the Fire
I will kindle my fire this morning,

In presence of the holy angels of heaven,
In presence of Ariel of the loveliest form,
In presence of Uriel of the myriad charms,
without malice, without jealousy, without envy,
without fear, without terror of any one under the sun,
But the holy Son of God to shield me.
God, kindle Thou in my heart within.[13]

Reflecting on these prayers, one gets a sense of the spiritual and material worlds flowing in and out of each other in a completely natural and unselfconscious way. In this tradition, according to Caithlín Matthews, blessing allows whatever is blessed to fully realise its innate potential.[14]

A Gift for Today

So what, if anything, does this pre-Celtic, Celtic and Celtic Christian tradition offer us as we journey into the twenty-first century? What gifts does it enfold for us?

I believe that this tradition with its core belief in the sacredness of the earth, embodied as it is with divine presence, can empower us to re-own a reverential attitude for the earth – an attitude that has been trivialised and lost in our times. By daring to enter into an understanding of the mind-set and wisdom of people who lived in much greater harmony with the natural world, we could learn how this may be translated into right relationship and right action in our daily lives.

Furthermore, to awaken fully to the possibility of other worlds around our world, unseen worlds which can and do influence the flux and flow of the visible world, would allow for an opening up to greater possibilities of 'being' in this life. To allow oneself to be open to the world of *muthos*, the world of imagination, as a way of being could, I believe, allow us a greater vision of life and a more fulfilled existence.

All of these gifts are there to be harvested by us in our time, in our unique way, as we, a Celtic people, draw on our past, so that we may move forward into the twenty-first century.

COLM CILLE
'A MAN FOR ALL SEASONS'

John J. Ó Ríordáin

By secular as well as religious standards, Colm Cille is one of the outstanding figures of Early Medieval Ireland. Speculation about his life, his reasons for leaving Ireland, the extent of his influence at home and abroad, and the extent of the Iona influence in Scotland, cannot detract from this fact. Nor can a case be made against his holiness on the grounds that he was not formally canonised by the Pope; Colm Cille lived hundreds of years prior to such formalities. When St Adomnán wrote his Life in the seventh century, it was specifically to establish for all and sundry that the first Abbot of Iona was a man who walked with God in a truly extraordinary and inspiring fashion. For fifteen hundred years the Christian community, particularly in Ireland and Scotland, has acknowledged this estimation of the man by invoking his intercession and keeping his memory green.[1]

Have I Something New to Write about Colm Cille?

Have I something new to write about Colm Cille? Nothing at all. Why do I write? To tell the story over again, because in Ireland as in so many other places, the oral Christian tradition is dying for the want of being told. This came home to me in two small but striking incidents in the recent past. When the attendant at a petrol station saw a sticker on my car, which read 'I love Iona', he asked inquiringly, 'Who is Iona?' The second incident occurred in a rural school which I visited during a parish mission. Among other things, I gave mention to the saint of the day, who happened to be a martyr. Just to be sure that we were speaking the same language, I interjected with the question: what is a martyr? After a brief pause a hand went up,

25

and on my nod of recognition, the reply came, 'one who buys and sells cattle, sir!'

Coming as he did when the Christian story in Ireland was only beginning to take root and shape, Colm Cille would have understood; as would Polycarp, the saint of that particular day – an eighty-six-year-old bishop and martyr who, from his hiding place in a farmyard shed, was sold at price, like an animal at the mart, before being taken away and killed.

Formation

In his childhood years Colm Cille was fostered after the Irish fashion. His guardian or foster-father, a local priest named Cruithnecán, not only taught the boy his letters and his prayers but gave him a shining, personal example of Christian living, so shining, indeed, that he too, like his young foster-child, is venerated as a saint of God. Kilmacrennan in County Donegal is named after him. There, beside his little church, is his burial place, or 'the place of his resurrection', as the Irish tradition so beautifully puts it.

Colm Cille's original name was Crimthann – Crimthann O'Donnell we would call him today. Because of his whole-hearted embrace of the Christian gospel and his habit of quiet visits to the little chapel, his friends and fellow-students dubbed him Colum Cille (Dove of the Church). Colum is a slight abbreviation of the Latin *Columba* (dove), which is itself still used as a variant of the saint's name. Irish Catholics invariably use the name Colm Cille; it combines the symbols of dove and church (*cill*), and is the more natural term in Gaelic.

Colm Cille was born with the proverbial 'silver spoon' in his mouth, AD 521 being the most reliable date. The world at his feet, the high kingship of Ireland within his grasp, but like St Paulinus of Nola (a multi-millionaire and Roman Consul in the previous century), he turned his back on it all for the sake of

Christ. Though differing in personality, both Paulinus and Colm Cille followed the same Gospel road and were proud, as Paulinus put it:

> To guard your altar through the silent night,
> And sweep your floor and keep your door by day,
> And watch your candles burn.[2]

The enthusiasm of Colm Cille wasn't confined to his youth, it characterised the man, too. It informed his years of study – scripture, theology, spirituality and folklore. We are told that he studied under St Finnian at the great school of Clonard in Meath, under one Gemman who is described as 'a Christian bard', and under the Rule of St Enda on the Aran Islands. It is said that he received the diaconate from St Finnian of Moville, in County Down, and was ordained to the priesthood by St Etchin at the monastery of Clonfad to the west of Kinnegad, County Westmeath.

An Enthusiastic Founder of Monasteries

Enthusiasm, which in the original Greek means 'full of God', also informed his promotion of the monastic ideal. There is no knowing how many monastic foundations he made, either in Ireland or outside of it. The *Martyrology of Donegal*, not stinting in praise of a native son, credits him with three hundred:

> Three hundred he measured, without fault,
> Of churches fair, 'tis true;
> And three hundred, lasting books
> Noble-bright he wrote.[3]

Durrow in Ireland and Iona in Scotland are his best authenticated foundations. Among the other sites thought to be authentic are Swords and Lambay Island in Dublin, Inchmore in Lough Gowna, County Longford, and, of course, his own beloved Derry; Doire Cholm Cille (Derry of Colm Cille). Kells in County Meath is best known because of its association with the book of that name, but there is doubt as to whether the foundation dates back to Colm Cille. It is not, however, the mere historical continuity but the continuity of inspiration that is of primary importance in linking such enterprises to a saint of God.

A Pilgrim for Christ's Sake

By the year 563 Colm Cille was forty-two. He had already done the work of a lifetime, and more than a lifetime, in Ireland. In his youth he had renounced the family inheritance, now he chose to go a step further and renounce his native land. Adomnán, his seventh-century biographer, says that the saint went into Britain to be 'a pilgrim for Christ's sake'.

In Early Christian Ireland, the greatest sacrifice and penance a monk could undertake, other than martyrdom, was voluntary exile, becoming a pilgrim for Christ's sake. Colm Cille, who wasn't in the habit of doing things by halves, took that penitential option. The late romantic legend attributing his exile to a row over a book has overshadowed this original Gospel inspiration.

His going must have been a source of sorrow to many, for he was not only a holy man, but was an admirable and attractive man in other ways. He was tall, handsome and affable, a poet of high accomplishment, a man born to rule, with a sweetness and power in his voice said to have been verging on the miraculous. He was too, what Erasmus later said of St Thomas More, a man 'born and made for friendship'. During his time there, the Inner Hebridean island of Iona, described by Adomnán as a 'small and remote island of the Britannic Ocean', became a Mecca for his sainted friends.

During the diocesan pilgrimage from Ardagh and Clonmacnoise to Iona in August 1997, Bishop Colm O'Reilly, quoting Bernard Lonergan, said, 'The best starting point for a prayer for pilgrimage is an openness to seeing life as a mystery, a place where God is actively present'. Bishop Colm went on to say:

> Life has questions to which we have no full answers. God is at work there, drawing us to himself. Mystery calls for wonder, for a sense of awe and reverence. This attitude does not come easily in a world that wants solutions, and seeks control of events. There is a desire to control through knowledge, through need for instant information and claiming the right to it, through seeking to be in charge of our destiny. Pilgrimage can be a help to seeing life as the journey that it is, whereas looking to false certainties can lead to elimination of the sense of mystery. All of life is a pilgrimage, a mystery of God leading, purifying, inspiring us, as we journey towards him.[4]

No one knew better than Colm Cille the truth of what he wrote in his creation hymn, the *Altus Prosator* (High Creator):

> The momentary glory of the kings of the present world, fleeting and tyrannical, is cast down at God's whim.[5]

Healer, Counsellor, Diplomat and Trouble-Shooter

Though he had abandoned the dominative power of a monarch, he freely exercised nutritive and healing power in his ministry, be it at the crowning of King Aidan on Iona, or while acting as diplomat and trouble-shooter at the Convention of Drum Ceat in County Derry in AD 575; or again, in the purifying of a polluted well, or the rehabilitation of a robber, or the counselling of a distraught woman in a bad marriage, or offering shelter and protection to a tired crane that had flown in from Ireland.

Even in the remoteness of Iona, he still felt the need to find a quiet place for prayer and regularly withdrew to a hermitage about a kilometre from the monastery.

On occasion he worked miracles, but never where simple good sense would suffice. Thus, he warned one of the brethren not to presume on God's providence by taking short-cuts across the open sea to Tiree, but to go the safer way by island-hopping. Though like the poet Aogán Ó Rathaille, he was reputed to have understood the language of birds, his relationship with nature was essential, practical and respectful.

Colm Cille chose exile, but his missionary career may have been thrust upon him by the circumstances in which he found himself. A similar development occurred in the exile of other saints. For example, St Fursa (a junior contemporary) went into the wilds of England to live as a hermit and be a pilgrim for Christ's sake, but on arrival he 'preached the Gospel as he always did'. Centuries later, on the Continent, the same pastoral spirit led the Irish monks and hermits to serve the local people and to become renowned for their attention to the sick – leading them to deepen and develop significantly the liturgy.

Death in Exile

After thirty-five years of exile, during which he evangelised widely in Scotland and made several important visits to Ireland, Colm Cille died peacefully on Iona. He was aware of the imminence of his death and the anticipation of it brought joy to his heart, for he was going to the one whom he had so faithfully loved and served from the days of his boyhood, when his friends affectionately dubbed him 'Dove of the Church'. And it was to the little church on Iona that he now hurried as the time for the night Office approached. Then a 'ball of light' (that strange Hebridean phenomenon known both in ancient and modern times, associated with death and birth) lit up the church as the monks streamed in for prayer. They found Colm Cille crumpled at the altar where he had fallen. His attendant, Brother Dermot, helped him raise his hand in blessing over the community, and thus he died. It was 9 June 597.

A Man for All Seasons

Like St Patrick before him, Colm Cille's abiding achievement was not simply in being a diplomat, an international negotiator, a trouble-shooter, or wonder-worker, but in the flowering of his great soul as an imitator of Christ, an example to inspire, a headline for every generation, 'a man for all seasons'.

On 9 June 1997, the fifteen hundredth anniversary of his death, I slipped quietly into his grave-shrine on Iona, at an hour when most people were fast asleep, and celebrated the Holy Eucharist. Two friends accompanied me on that holy night, but I suspect there was a third!

BRIGIT: MUIRE NA NGAEL (MARY OF THE GAEL)
THE ETERNAL FEMININE
IN THE CELTIC TRADITION

Padraigín Clancy

What is Happening?

Ireland in the late twentieth century sees a new turning towards matters Celtic. Central in this is a new exploration of Brigit, 'Muire na nGael' (Mary of the Gael). In the past decade there have been new studies on her (notably Ó Catháin and Ó Duinn)[1] and a marked proliferation in the number of workshops, conferences and retreats concerning her. Many of these are conducted around her feast day – St Brigit's Day, 1 February.

There is, for example, the annual *Féile Bríde* in Kildare, a combined project of AFRI[2] and the Brigidine Sisters, which attracts an international audience who are committed, in the spirit of Brigit, to issues of poverty and justice. There is also the annual convocation of the 'Institute for Feminism and Religion' which brings together large numbers of women in Dublin, Belfast and Galway to draw from 'the well' of her tradition. The decade has also seen the revitalising of older festivals such as *Éigse na Brídeoige* in County Kerry, and there is a renewed interest in the quietly continued legacy of unbroken folk tradition which is still found in customs such as the *Brídeog*, *Brat* and *Cros Bríde*, practised countrywide in honour of her feast. In fact, this folklorist can confess, each springtime, to being scarcely able to meet the demands for lectures, seminars and media input on Brigit, whether at local or national level.

This happening sparks a reappraisal of Brigit and raises fundamental questions such as: Who is Brigit? What does she represent? What are the various elements in her tradition? Why the renewed interest in her? and What exactly is it that Irish people in the late twentieth century are finding enriching about her tradition?

Celtic Goddess and Christian Saint

Brigit comes down to us in Ireland as both a pre-Christian Celtic goddess of ancient lineage and a Christian saint of the fifth century. As Mac Cana tells us, the two Brigits are inextricably linked.[3] In fact, they have been so finely intermeshed that it would be impossible to understand the significance of the cult of the saint without knowing the story of the pre-Christian goddess. Just as in many respects it would be impossible to understand the New Testament without the Old, the holy woman of fifth-century Kildare and the traditions surrounding her can only be understood with a knowledge of her pre-Christian ancestor. Spanning such a wide epoch, it may be said that Brigit represents the eternal feminine in Irish folk tradition. It is no surprise, therefore, that folklore has bestowed on her the epithet 'Muire na nGael' (Mary of the Gael).

Brigit: Pre-Christian Celtic Goddess

The term Brigit is taken in Old Irish to mean 'the exalted one' and from what we know of the Celtic goddess she was the foremost goddess or 'sovereign' among the pre-Christian Celtic pantheon.[4] Evidence suggests that there was an extensive cult surrounding her. Placenames extending back into pre-Christian times, such as *Topar Brigte* (modern Irish *tobar* /well) or *Cell Brigte* (modern Irish *cill* /church) are found countrywide, but most particularly in the Leinster region.[5]

Bearing in mind that in the insular Celtic tradition, manuscript evidence is confined to Christian times, one of our earliest direct references to the pre-Christian Brigit is found in

the glossary of a ninth-century monk of Cashel, Cormac mac
Cuillenáin. He tells us:

> Brigit i.e. daughter of the Dagda. That is Brigit woman
> of learning i.e. a goddess whom the _filid_ [poets/seers]
> worshipped. For her protecting care was very great and
> very wonderful. So they called her goddess of poets. Her
> sisters were Brigit woman of healing and Brigit woman of
> smith-work, daughters of the Dagda from whose names
> among all the Irish a goddess used to be called Brigit.[7]

Here Brigit appears in typical Celtic trinitarian form
possessing various qualities of the archetypal feminine. As
protector and inspiration of poets she embodies the spirit of
wisdom. She also embodies the spirit of Gaelic/Irish sovereignty
– when we recollect the centrality of the role of the poet in
Gaelic society and that poetry as Carney tells us 'was so closely
woven into the fabric of political Gaeldom that without it that
society could not continue to exist unless by changing its very
essence'.[7] Brigit therefore is the divine Sofia (inspiration) that
lies at the heart of Gaelic society.

Mac Cuillenáin's reference also intimately connects her with
healing and with the smith's craft – a vital craft among the
Celts, whose material remains show us that 'society was
endowed with technology and craft skills unsurpassed in
Europe until the eighteenth century AD'.[8]

These aspects of the Celtic goddess Brigit – protection,
healing, wisdom, as well as others such as fertility and fecundity
– recur throughout the written Lives of St Brigit and are found
in the folk custom and belief surrounding the saint. In fact,
most of our knowledge of the pre-Christian Brigit can be
gleaned from the tradition surrounding the saint or holy
woman of fifth-century Kildare.

Brigit and the Legacy of the Old European Goddess

Before examining the lives and lore of St Brigit, it is important to realise the wider European context surrounding her pre-Christian ancestor. Marija Gimbutas sees the Irish goddess Brigit as one of the descendants of the Old European Goddess, whose existence is attested archaeologically from earliest times. Gimbutas writes:

> Greek Artemis Eileithya, Thracinn Bendis, Venetic Rhetia, and Roman Diana as well as the living fate in European folk beliefs – particularly the Baltic Laima and the Irish Brigit – are unquestionable descendants of the pre-historic life-giving goddess.... The historic and pre-historic life-giver was a mistress of mountains, stones, waters, forests and animals, an incarnation of the mysterious powers of nature. Being an owner of wells, springs and healing waters she was a miraculous bestower of health.... She was the guardian of the well-being of the family and from paleolithic times must have been considered to be the ancestress and progenetrix of the family or clan.[9]

The basic dynamic which Gimbutas sees the Old European archetype as possessing is that of giver of life and yielder of death, and no less importantly regeneratrix (regenerator of life). She is not confined to earth but depicted throughout the universe as cosmic mother. She is not in original form married to a God but instead is parthenogenetic (self-generating). Images which cluster around her throughout art include spirals, coiling symbols, circles. Mythological depictions of her include deer, bear, cow, snake, bee and various bird types.[10]

An appreciation of the *wholism* of the Old European Goddess tradition and its legacy is vital in understanding the multifaceted aspects which are all part of the tradition surrounding Brigit, Muire na nGael.

St Brigit: The Written Lives

Our earliest accounts of St Brigit in the manuscript tradition are three Lives written in the seventh century.[11] One of these, Cogitosus' *Vita Brigitae,* is the oldest Life we have of any saint in Ireland.[12] These Lives are written in typical hagiographical form and consist of a panegyric on the saint rather than a linear life.

Our school books, therefore, which tell us with absolute certainty that Brigit was born in 450 in Faughart, County Louth, cannot be taken as being historically accurate. Regarding a linear account at best, we can be sure that she lived sometime at the end of the fifth and the beginning of the sixth century. Where exactly she was born we do not know but it was evidently somewhere in the Leinster region. That she was a woman of the Fotharta sept, one of the minor dynasties under the Uí Dhúnlainge of Leinster, also seems certain (the term 'Fothatha' may explain the connection with Faughart). That her father was named Dubhtach and her mother Broicsech, that her monastery at Kildare commanded considerable stature in the Leinster region, and that she inherited the cult of her pre-Christian ancestor, we can also take as being accurate.

While they do not directly tell us much about Brigit, these early Lives are nonetheless indirectly helpful and are most useful as early historical documents. They provide us with: a) an insight into the political life of early Ireland, in particular the context in which Brigit's monastery at Kildare operates; b) an insight into the position and role of women in early Ireland; c) an insight into the structure, layout and activity of an early monastery; and d) the motifs attached to the saint provide us with further knowledge of the pre-Christian goddess Brigit.

As each of these themes widens our knowledge of Brigit, it is worth addressing each briefly.

a) Seventh-Century Ireland and the Three Patrons: Patrick, Brigit and Colm Cille

Ireland in the seventh century was little different from Ireland in the late twentieth century, with struggles for power and control occurring in political and ecclesiastical life. The monasteries at Kildare, Armagh and Iona each had a network of affiliated monasteries under them. By the seventh century, each was aspiring to overall predominance in Ireland. That century therefore saw a propaganda war between the three – a proliferation of the Lives of the three saints associated with them, the three we now refer to in the Roman Catholic Church as the three patrons: Patrick, Brigit and Colm Cille.

History has shown us that the Legend of Patrick and Armagh prevailed and Armagh remains the primary see of the main Christian Churches in Ireland to the present day. The important point in this context is that the three Lives of Brigit indicate to us that the monastery at Kildare commanded considerable stature and influence in early Ireland. In what is clearly an exaggeration but nonetheless an indication of the stature of Brigit's monastery, Cogitosus claims:

> It is head of almost all the Irish Churches with supremacy over all the monasteries of the Irish and its *paruchia* extends over the whole land of Ireland, reaching from sea to sea....[13]

b) The Status of Women in Early Ireland: Brigit, the Early Feminist, Defying Her Parents to Become a Nun

As regards the status of women, the early (and later) Lives tell us that Brigit defies her parents to become a nun. This theme recurs in the Lives of female saints in Ireland. It reminds us that the Church in early Ireland offered women an alternative to that which Gaelic/Celtic society traditionally expected of them, i.e. marriage.

In a recent study Máirín Nic Eoin has shown that the wholistic status accorded women in Celtic mythology is not translated into Gaelic/Celtic society.[14] Lest we get too carried away, therefore, with the wonders of the Celtic tradition, it is no harm to remind ourselves of the legal status accorded a woman under Gaelic or Brehon law:

> ...her father has charge over her when she is a girl, her husband when she is a wife, her sons when she is a widowed woman with children, her kin when she is 'a woman of the kin' (i.e. with no other guardian), the church when she is a woman of the church (i.e. a nun). She is not capable of sale or purchase or contract or transaction without the authorization of one of her superiors.[15]

In an episode in one seventh-century Life, Brigit is depicted as having accidentally been consecrated a bishop. While this may or may not be literally true, its inclusion further attests to the status of Kildare and of the woman Brigit as its chief administrator.[16]

c) The Monastery at Kildare

That there was a monastery in Kildare of considerable size is attested to archaeologically and historically. It is depicted as being very ornate, somewhat like Eastern Orthodox Christian Churches. The walls of the cathedral church, we are told, are 'painted with pictures and covered with wall-hangings', and Brigit and Conleth (the archbishop resident at Kildare):

rest in tombs adorned with a refined profusion of gold, silver, gems and precious stones with gold and silver chandeliers hanging from above and different images presenting a variety of carvings and colours.[17]

The monastery contains lay and religious of both sexes, safely separated by partitions, as Cogitosus makes sure to tell us, yet all praying together in one vast basilica:

> And so, in one vast basilica, a large congregation of people of varying status, rank, sex and local origin, with partitions placed between them, prays to the omnipotent Master, differing in status, but one in spirit....[18]

Typical of its day in early Christian Ireland, the monastery functions as a refuge or a safe haven for the poor, the sick and fugitives seeking justice. It espouses most especially the Celtic Christian ethos of Hospitality; all are received with equal care and attention, from the starving animal to the bishop.

Brigit is portrayed as an exemplar of Christian virtue. She is a miraculous healer and comforter of the sick, a possessor of wisdom in making discerned decisions, a supporter of those suffering injustice, generous to the poor, kind to animals, and her mind is continuously turned towards God in prayer.

d) St Brigit: Inheritor of the Celtic Goddess Archetypes

The images of St Brigit in the written Lives abound with the archetypes of the goddess. She is depicted as possessing the ability to control nature, which has obvious ancient associations with the role of cosmological mother. We are told 'that the whole of nature, beasts, cattle and birds, was subjected to her power'.[19]

We are also told that she has the ability to milk the same cow three times in the one day. The cow is an ancient symbol of the feminine and milk represents its nurturing aspects. In Irish folklore, milk is also seen as a source of wisdom or poetry – these motifs represent various aspects of the archetypal feminine and the legacy of the Celtic goddess.[20]

The connection with the goddess is most especially emphasised by the fact that the date given, in the written Lives, for St Brigit's death (1 February) is one that is associated with the pre-Christian festival of *imbolc* (parturition/birth). This was a spring festival connected with the pre-Christian goddess.[21]

Brigit in Irish Folklore

It is in the area of folk tradition that Brigit is perhaps best understood – and her tradition kept alive. As folklore tends towards the inclusion rather than the exclusion of that which previously existed, the two Brigits (goddess and saint) come together in folk custom and belief.

Calendar Custom

Many customs centre around St Brigit's feast day (1 February) and have an ancient provenance. They represent what could be described as a form of folk liturgy.[22] Most have to do with the ritual bringing in of new life (the spring) into the home. They invoke the protection, healing and fertile powers of the divine through St Brigit. Although no longer as widely found, they are still practised in parts of Ireland and Scotland. Some elements of the tradition include the following:

Brigit: Regenerator of Life

St Brigit's Day marks the first day of spring in the Celtic reckoning of the year. Typical of many descriptions held in the archive of the Department of Irish Folklore, an account from County Clare tells us:

New Life is infused into the earth on St Brigit's Day and this is a token to commence manual labours on the farm. The first shining of the sun comes on this day and clothes are put out on the walls or bushes for their first 'airing' or 'sunning'. The linnet is called *Beag Éan Bríde* (the little Bird of Brigit) – it begins to sing on her day. The dandelion is called *Beárnán Bríde* (the serrated flower of Brigit) – it begins to flower on her day. People pray to Brigit to give them good crops.... Brigit is very much associated with cows and milk....[23]

Clearly this portrayal of St Brigit is as cosmological mother. She is depicted as the regenerator of life – the unseen force behind the cycle of the seasons and the cycle of life. She is the hag of *Samhain* (Halloween) transformed into the virgin of spring. She represents the victory of light and life over darkness and death.

Brigit is not only associated with being midwife to the cycle of the seasons but also to the human lifecycle. In Scottish and Irish folk prayer, Brigit's aid is traditionally invoked by women in childbirth. Here, the lore of St Brigit echoes the cult of the Celtic goddess and represents ancient aspects of the divine feminine.

Cros Bríde/St Brigit's Cross

The great emblem of the Brigitine tradition is the cross made of rushes. Rushes are traditionally laid down in the birthing place in Irish folk custom and are, therefore, intimately connected with new life; Ó Catháin suggests that this may be why they are used in the Brigitine symbol.[24]

The crosses are traditionally made on the eve of the feast. The rushes are picked and ritually brought into the dwelling-house after dark. A member of the household customarily pretends to be Brigit and, knocking on the entrance to the dwelling-house door, says words such as *'An bhfuil fáilte roimh Bríd?'* (Is Brigit welcome?) or *'Gabhaigí ar bhur nglúine, fosclaigí bhur súile, agus ligigí isteach Bríd!'* (Go on your knees, open your eyes, and admit Brigit!), and the response, often led by the woman of the house, is with words such as *'Is é beatha! Is é beatha! Is é beatha na mná uaisle!'* (Welcome! Welcome! Welcome to the holy woman!)[25]

The crosses are customarily blessed with holy water and placed above the inside of the entrance door in the dwelling-house and in outhouses. They are said to invoke the power of St Brigit's protection from sickness and fire.

Various types of crosses (three-armed, four-armed, diamond and interwoven) are found throughout the country.[26] These symbols occur in identical form in prehistoric stone carvings throughout Europe. They are understood to be ancient symbols of the Old European goddess – thus it would seem that our ever-popular St Brigit's Cross has a very ancient provenance.[27]

Brat Bríde/St Brigit's Mantle or Cloak

The *brat* is a relic of the saint. It refers to a piece of cloth (usually small in size) which is customarily left outside the dwelling-house on the eve of her feast. It is held that Brigit blesses the dew on that eve and thereby endows the *brat* with healing and curative powers. Representing the wholism of the Brigitine tradition, the brat is multi-purpose. It is believed to be efficacious in the healing of headaches, in protecting virginity in young girls, in increasing fertility in women and in aiding parturition in animals and women.

The cloth used in the *brat* can be anything from an ordinary piece of ribbon to a special silk. Some informants relate that they use the same piece of cloth each year, while others get a new piece and burn the old. The cloth used is generally white, blue or red in colour. White and blue are the Marian colours, and red traditionally provides protection from the fairies.

The miraculous powers of St Brigit's Mantle/Cloak are well renowned in Irish folklore. Legend has it that, having been told by the local king that she could have as much land for her monastery at Kildare as her cloak would cover, Brigit placed it on the ground, and it spread and spread, providing her with a large domain.

A popular blessing invoking the protection of Brigit's Mantle, found throughout Ireland, is *'Brat Bríde Ort'* (The Mantle of Brigit Upon You).[28]

Brídeog/Ceremonial Image of St Brigit

This refers to the custom of carrying an effigy of Brigit from door to door in some parts of Ireland. It is customarily done by young boys and girls (sometimes girls only). Brigit is welcomed into the home and the children are given a gift (nowadays money) in return for their visit. It is a form of seasonal, communal luck perambulation. It is still carried out in places such as County Clare, County Kerry, Inis Meáin and Inis Oírr, the Aran Islands, County Galway.[29]

Iasc Beo/Live Shellfish

Another custom still found in Árainn, Inis Mór, the Aran Islands, is that of bringing live shellfish into the home on St Brigit's day. These are placed in the four corners of the house and are said to increase its prosperity in the coming year.

The shellfish used include limpets and barnacles. These have a parthenogenetic significance. This custom may represent an ancient link with the cosmic aspects of the mythological goddess, Brigit.[30]

Crios Bríde/St Brigit's Girdle

This custom is no longer practised. A girdle representing that of the saint was traditionally made from straw. It was carried about from house to house in a village by the young boys. Occupants of each house stepped through the *crios* while reciting a special prayer invoking St Brigit's protection.[31] Poet Seamas Heaney writes delightfully about the practice of stepping through the *crios*:

> the open they came into by these moves
> Stood opener, hoops came off the world,
> They could feel the February air....[32]

Folk Legends of St Brigit

Legends abound portraying St Brigit as provider for the sick and the poor. As Christ is represented in Irish folklore in the guise of the poor person or stranger, so too is Brigit. If the occupants of a house being visited are not generous, they are duly reprimanded when Brigit discloses her identity. These legends are used as parables in Irish tradition to teach Christian values.

St Brigit and Our Lady

Brigit and Mary tend to appear together in story and prayer throughout Irish folklore. It would seem to have been the ordinary people's way of integrating Our lady alongside their own Brigit. One popular tradition has it that Brigit was the midwife at Jesus' birth. This image again has echoes of the divine cosmological mother birthing creation. St Brigit is depicted as birthing the cosmic Christ.

Folk Prayers Invoking St Brigit

St Brigit is invoked in many folk prayers. She is especially associated with the hearth fire and is traditionally invoked by the woman of the house when banking up the fire at night.[33] I received this version of the prayer from my friend and neighbour in Árainn, Nan Ellen Hernon, recently deceased (*Go ndéana Dia grásta uirthi*):

Coiglím an tine seo mar a choigil Críost cách,
Muire máthair an tí agus Bríd ina lár,
An ceathrar aingeal is airde i gCathair na nGrást
Ag cumhdach an tí seo anocht is go brách.

Keep in this fire as Christ keeps us all in,
Mary mother of the house and Brigit at its centre,
The four highest angels in the city of God,
Be protecting this house tonight and forever.

The hearth fire is the symbol of the life and spirit of the home family and community. In Christian teaching, fire represents the flame of the Holy Spirit and is the feminine principle.

The monastery at Kildare is reputed to have had a fire burning in it from earliest times. Scholars suggest that it is likely it was originally a pagan fire temple dedicated to the goddess Brigit, which then became Christianised in honour of the saint.[34]

Brigit: Inspiration for Today

Today Brigit is proving a new source of inspiration in the religious experience of Irish people. I see this as being significant in the following ways:

1) Part of the Return to the Celtic Tradition

The return to Brigit is part of the general return to the religious inspiration of the Celtic tradition. The thirst among people of all walks of life for that which can be spiritually life-giving in their own tradition is clear to me from the many seminars I have given around Ireland. Knowledge of our own faith-story and of the lives of Irish holy men and women of previous generations is proving to be a source of inspiration. This, I find, is felt in equal measure among lay and religious. Many of the latter, while familiar with the lives of continental saints, have little knowledge, because of inadequate training, of their own tradition. Since Vatican Two, the interplay between faith and culture is also acknowledged by the Roman Catholic Church – it encourages acculturation, which is essentially the encountering of Christ through the indigenous culture.

Brigit has the weight of organic tradition behind her – one that spans pre-Christian and Christian times in Ireland. There is hardly a district that does not have some devotion to her in the form of holy well, local church or calendar custom. This kind of tradition provides a solid context for the teaching of gospel values at local level.

2) An Ecumenical Appeal

St Brigit, being a pre-Reformation Irish holy woman, belongs to all Christian Churches on the island. The cathedral church of St Brigit in Kildare is at present under the guardianship of the Church of Ireland. This community works closely with other denominations in facilitating the remembering of Brigit.

3) Telling 'Her-Story'

It is perhaps as an inspiration for women that Brigit's influence is being most profoundly felt in Ireland today. Labouring under the weight of *his-story*, women (and men) welcome the chance to redress the imbalance by telling *her-story*. The image of the saint as a strong woman, in charge of a large monastery with a network of smaller monasteries under her; the image of a woman riding out on her chariot, settling disputes, making wise decisions, befriending the sick, poor and downtrodden – have universal appeal.

The archetypes of the feminine also provide inspiration as women (and men) struggle to find the sovereign, the wise, the nurturer, the powerful within themselves and within society. There is a virgin (pure mind), a mother (nurturer and birther) and a crone (wise woman, sufferer, endurer) in each of us. There is also its potential shadow (a puritanical mind, a smotherer, and a killer). Brigit as regenerator of life represents the transformation of the shadow in the feminine mysteries, of the Celtic tradition, and is therefore the *Brigeoit*, i.e. 'the exalted one'.

A knowledge of Brigit also helps towards a greater understanding of Mary and the centrality of her place in Irish spirituality. An embracing of the archetypes of the feminine through the Brigitine tradition can help the embracing of Mary in all her aspects as Virgin Mother and Crone (Mother of Good Counsel). An over-concentration on the virginal aspect of Mary and the excessive petrification of that archetype has meant that some of the riches of the wholism of the Marian tradition have not been fully recognised.

The telling of Brigit's story is also important in the relating of the lives of other female saints in Ireland. The stories of Ita, Gobnait, Samthann, etc all need to be told and retold simply because they are not widely known. Many of the images and motifs attached to these women represent both ancient archetypes and the eternal feminine in the Celtic tradition.

Brigit also has counterparts in other European countries. Female saints, some of the same name, personify by their lives the archetypes of the divine feminine.

4) Re-vitalising Religious Celebration: Familial and Communal

The customs and stories surrounding St Brigit and her feast day are being used to add 'new life' and vitality to liturgy. The holy well – intimately connected with Brigit – can be a focus for creative worship, as a source of life-giving water, a symbol of baptism, a place of healing and revelation. The various elements in the occasion – rushes, *cros, brat, brídeog* – can help creative

Christian celebration. Stories attached to Brigit can also be used as parables to teach gospel values.

The value of many of these folk customs is that they are centred in the dwelling-house and the local community. In an age where familial and communal prayer is rapidly declining, these old customs can revitalise faith expression in the home and community.

An Enduring Tradition

In conclusion, we can say that Brigit represents an enduring tradition. As primordial divine feminine, she is as ancient as the hills and wells of Ireland. The woman who was abbess at Kildare embodied these divine archetypes in a life dedicated to Christ. As we enter the third millennium, our challenge may be to join with Brigit, Muire na nGael, in birthing the Christ consciousness in Ireland in a new way.

> *A Naoimh Bhríd, a Mhuire na nGael, guí orainn!*
> *A Naoimh Bhríd, a Mhuire na nGael, scaoil tharainn do bhrat!*

> St Brigit, Mary of the Gael, pray for us!
> St Brigit, Mary of the Gael, surround us with your mantle!

THE BIBLE, THE DESERT AND THE
CELTIC TRADITION

Marcus Losack

Introduction

In the *Life of St Paul the Hermit,* published by St Jerome, there
is a story about the meeting of St Paul and St Anthony in the
Desert.[1] Paul of Thebes (known locally as St Bola) was one of
the first hermits in the Egyptian desert. Tradition says he
befriended two lions and was fed each day by a raven, which
brought him half a loaf of bread. His tunic was made from palm
leaves and he was renowned for his asceticism.

One day, St Anthony went out to meet St Paul in the
wilderness. On that occasion the raven brought a whole loaf of
bread, sufficient to feed the two saints. An icon of this meeting
can be found today at St Anthony's Monastery in Egypt, where
the teachings and traditions of the desert are preserved in the
Coptic (Egyptian) monasteries.

In his book on the Irish high crosses, Peter Harbison notes
that inscriptions of this meeting between St Paul and St
Anthony can be found carved in stone on at least eighteen of
the Irish high crosses.[2] What purpose did these inscriptions have
in the teachings of the early Irish monasteries? How did this
story find its way to Ireland and what significance did the desert
have in the lives of the early Irish saints? To explore the
appearance of these inscriptions in Ireland and related questions
concerning the origins of Irish monasticism, we will examine
and reflect on the relationship between the Bible, the desert and
the Celtic tradition.

The Desert in the Old Testament: A Physical and Spiritual Experience

In the Old Testament, the desert is central to the Jewish experience of God. Ken Leech, one of the great writers of the Anglican Church this century, has said:

> It was in the desert, barren, unpredictable and surprising that the people of God were to learn the lesson and privilege of complete dependence on God in the simplicity of naked faith.... It was in the desert, in the howling wastes of wilderness, that Israel found her identity as a people of God and where God was revealed to her in the desert.[3]

The desert was not just a physically barren place, it was also a spiritually barren place, which forced the people to reflect on their faith and trust in God. The forty years' pilgrimage in the Sinai was remembered as a time of testing and spiritual formation, from which the Israelites emerged with a deeper sense of their own identity and a closer relationship with God. God's promises were manifested in the desert. Yet there was a paradox in the desert experience. The desert was a place of deprivation and hardship, with loneliness, temptation and inward struggle, but at the same time it was a place of revelation and of a deeper encounter with God. God challenged and sustained those who persevered in the pilgrimage through the desert. Deuteronomy tells us that God was revealed more deeply in the darkness of the desert experience and that God actually went out into the desert to befriend Jacob:

> He found him [Jacob] in a desert land, in a waste and howling void. He protected and trained him and guarded him as the apple of his eye (Deuteronomy 32:10).

The Exodus from Egypt provided the foundation for the development of a spirituality of the desert. In this archetypal pilgrimage, which was both a physical and a spiritual journey, the Israelites crossed the Red Sea into the wilderness of Sinai, where they were very thirsty but could find only the bitter waters of Marah to drink (Exodus 15:22). There was bitterness in the water and there was bitterness in their souls too, with much anguish in the community, threatened by death and not knowing where the necessities for survival would come from. But this frightening experience was followed almost immediately by discovery of the springs of refreshment, which provided relief from their thirst.

The murmuring and complaining to Moses and to God reached its great climax in that terrible 'cry of the soul', when the Israelites said that it would have been better if Moses had left them in Egypt, where they were slaves but at least had plenty to eat, rather than bring them out into the desert to die. Again, at that moment of deep despair and darkness, God appeared as glory in the cloud and there was provision of the heavenly *manna* (Exodus 16:13).

The Desert in the New Testament: The Formation of Jesus

In the New Testament, the desert was a very significant place for Jesus and had a profound influence on his own spiritual formation. After his baptism, Jesus was 'driven by the Spirit' into the wilderness, where he fasted for forty days and forty nights (Matthew 4:11). During this time Jesus wrestled with darkness and despair, but was able to find reconciliation and a much clearer sense of his own identity and purpose. Having gained strength and discernment from Scripture, he was able to overcome the issues he was wrestling with and have a clearer understanding of the future course of his ministry. For him, the ultimate desert experience was at Golgotha, in the suffering and darkness of the Cross, which he endured before his resurrection from the dead.

The story of the Transfiguration and the forty days and forty nights in the wilderness connects Jesus with the desert traditions associated with Moses and Elijah. At Golgotha, his terrible cry of the soul 'My God, My God, why have you forsaken me?' echoes the cries of the Israelites in Sinai.

Early Christian Desert Spirituality

In the third century AD, one of the great theologians and teachers in the early Church took the biblical stories and the experiences of the early saints and martyrs and interpreted them in the context of a spirituality of the desert. Origen (AD 184-254) describes spiritual formation in terms of the journey through the wilderness. The spiritual progress of the soul is described as a pilgrimage through the desert, through various stages of trial, temptation and difficulty which, when they are overcome, lead to the attainment of holiness. Origen develops this spirituality of the desert using allegorical interpretations of Scripture, which focus on the pilgrimage through the wilderness to the Promised Land as an image of the soul's quest for wholeness and salvation:

> Before [the soul] arrives at perfection, it dwells in the wilderness where it is trained in the commandments of God and where its faith is tested by temptations. And when it conquers each temptation and its faith has been proved, it comes to another and it passes, as it were from one stage to another. So, when it proceeds through the different temptations of life and faith one by one, it is said to pass through stages through which an increase in virtue and holiness is achieved... until the soul arrives at the goal of its pilgrimage... namely the highest summit of virtue

and crosses the river of God and receives the heritage promised to it (Origen: Homily XXVII on Numbers).[4]

Whilst Origen was not the only writer dealing with this subject, his teachings contributed significantly to the development of a desert spirituality. A growing interest in the teachings of the desert and the examples of the desert saints, encouraged men and women to leave their homes and seek a refuge in the wilderness, to practice asceticism. By the time Christianity became the established religion of the Empire, after The Edict of Toleration issued by Constantine in 315, the desert had become a refuge for thousands of people seeking guidance from hermits, who had developed reputations for great holiness and wisdom. These teachings of the desert burst dramatically into the life of the Church in the fourth century, with the rise of *desert monasticism* in Egypt, Syria and Palestine and the wisdom of those who became known as the 'Desert Fathers and Mothers'.[5]

Early Christian Ireland and Egyptian Monasticism

The teachings of the desert must have reached Ireland at an early stage, before the end of the fifth century. There was significant contact between the Irish Church and the Churches in Gaul, as well as in Britain, where the desert tradition was known through the publication of Athanasius' *Life of Anthony* (translated into Latin by Evagrius) and the writings of John Cassian (AD 365-435), who had visited Egypt and been a disciple of the desert saints for many years.

It would be interesting to know whether any of the teachings and traditions of the desert came to Ireland more directly, for example through the journeys and travels of the eastern monks. In his book, *Monks and Monasteries of the Egyptian Deserts,*[6] Otto Meinardus notes that the extent of the influence of

Egyptian monasticism in Britain and Ireland has yet to be fully determined. We know that the Egyptian Monastic Rule was prevalent in Britain before the coming of Augustine. There is an intriguing reference in the Book of Leinster which mentions that seven Egyptian monks were buried in Díseart Ulaid, which is in County Antrim in the north of Ireland.[7]

It has also been noted that there are strong similarities between some Irish and Egyptian monastic customs, including for example the tradition of singing the psalms, known as the 'three fifties', which is a characteristic of both Churches.[8] The Stowe Missal, the oldest missal of the Irish Church, refers to Egyptian anchorites of the fourth century.

The Quest for Holiness in the Celtic Christian Tradition

The marked emphasis on asceticism, pilgrimage and the heroic quest for knowledge of the sacred, which was prominent in the desert tradition, was very attractive to the Celts and had a profound impact on the development of Celtic Christianity. This is nowhere more apparent than in the lives of the early Irish saints, which are characterised by a deep love of asceticism and the quest for holiness.

Following the example of the Desert Fathers and Mothers, many of the early Irish saints went to isolated places in the countryside, sometimes on remote islands or on the mainland in places like Glendalough, where they could practise asceticism in communion with God and with nature, in the solitude of the Irish wilderness or 'Celtic desert'. Those who built the monastery on Skellig Michael must have been driven by the same pioneering spirit as the Egyptian desert saints, when they crossed the sea in their coracles to this rocky wasteland.

On the Aran islands, St Enda was renowned for the strictness and discipline of his monastic rule. Enda had travelled in Europe and had been influenced by Martin of Tours, David of Wales and Ninian of Whithorn, who all practised a severe form of asceticism akin to that of the desert monasteries in Egypt.

In the sixth century, St Kevin crossed over the Wicklow Mountains to Glendalough, where he lived as a hermit. He built a cell overlooking the Upper Lake and survived by eating nuts and berries from the forest. The remains of this cell can be seen to the present day. The area around the Upper Lake is known as Díseart Chaoimhín (Kevin's Desert).[9] The term *díseart* or *dysert*, denoting a monastic settlement or hermitage, appears frequently in placenames in Ireland and Scotland.

St Columba journeyed across the 'desert of the ocean' in search of 'the place of Resurrection'. He is famous as a founder of monasteries rather than as a hermit. His monastery at Iona in Scotland was based on the model of the desert monasteries and the nearby Island of Hinba provided opportunities for greater seclusion, fasting and penance. Resembling Jacob in the desert, Columba slept alone in a beehive hut, with a stone for his pillow. Columban monasteries, in fact, acted as guardians for the desert tradition; through a network of abbots and abbesses who held autonomous authority in their monasteries, they reflected a model of Church and religious community that was different from the Roman model, which was based on an episcopal hierarchy.

St Cuthbert is one of the great hermit saints of Britain, and he is still remembered with much affection in Northumbria and the north-east of England. He was trained as a monk in the Celtic tradition, which had come to Lindisfarne from Iona. He built his cell on one of the deserted islands of the Inner Farne and practised an austere form of asceticism, including the 'cross vigil', popular among many Celtic saints, which involved standing for hours in the cold water of the sea with arms outstretched in the shape of the cross or sacred tree. Cuthbert tried to heal conflicts that had arisen between the Roman and Celtic parties, manifested so divisively at the Synod of Whitby in 664 CE. His whole life was inspired by the teachings of the desert and his tomb at Durham Cathedral is an important place of pilgrimage today for those who seek to learn from the traditions of the early Celtic Churches in Britain.[10]

Céili Dé Reform

The teachings of the desert and the practice of asceticism formed one of the main characteristics of the *Céili Dé* Reform (700-900 CE), which had a significant impact on the Irish Church in the eighth century. The leaders of the Céili Dé (such as St Maelruan of Tallaght and Aengus the Culdee) were seeking a return to the ideals of the early Irish saints and the teachings of the desert, including the practice of asceticism, which had become lax as monasteries became more established and wealthy. Like the Desert Monastic Movement which arose in Egypt, Syria and Palestine in the fourth century, the Céili Dé Reform may have developed in part as a protest against the wealth and worldliness that had appeared in the Irish Church, which had led to political and economic corruption, with spirituality compromised.

The Céili Dé Reform was noted for its asceticism and holiness, with a simplicity in lifestyle that reached out to the poor and needy. The fruits of the Reform could also be seen in the return to the disciplines of the desert spiritual tradition, which led to the flowering of Celtic art and calligraphy, so characteristic of the Irish Church in the period from 700 to 900 CE. The Céili Dé Reform contributed substantially to the growth of insular monastic literature and especially nature poetry, which characterised this very creative period in the Irish Church.[11]

Desert Spirituality in the Art of Irish High Crosses

Some of the best examples of the strong links between the desert and the Celtic tradition appear outside the written Lives of the Irish saints and can be seen on the magnificent stone carvings that adorn several Irish high crosses. Themes from the desert appear in prominent positions on the crosses, which date from about the ninth century. On the North Cross at Castledermot, there is a fine carving of the meeting of St Anthony and St Paul in the wilderness. At nearby Moone, there is a whole series of carvings with themes from the desert, including the Temptation of St Anthony and stories which can be found in the Life of St Anthony by Athanasius and the Life of St Paul the Hermit, written by St Jerome. There is also a very interesting and beautiful carving of a six-headed beast or animal figure with tri-spirals emanating from its belly. This could be a symbol of the monster or demons which the hermits encountered during their temptations in the desert.[12] This carving has a profound symbolism, inviting us to reflect on the inward and spiritual struggles that characterised the hermit's experience of God.

It is probable that the specific teachings or stories associated with the desert which were portrayed in these carvings, were interpreted and explained for the students and pilgrims who visited them, as part of the spiritual guidance and instruction given by the Irish monks. A reference from the Life of Columba in the Book of Lismore describes three ways in which people are called to a knowledge of God. In this case the teachings of the desert are given priority even over the scriptures:

> Now there are three ways in which we are summoned to a knowledge of the Lord and to the membership of His family. This is the first way; the urging and kindling by the divine grace to serve the Lord after the example of

Paul and of Anthony, the monk, and of the other faithful monks who used to serve God there in Egypt.[13]

Decline of the Desert Spiritual Tradition in Ireland

By the time the Normans arrived in Ireland in the twelfth century, the Golden Age of Celtic Christianity was largely over. Substantial elements of this desert tradition must have survived well into the Middle Ages, perhaps until the destructions of Cromwell in the seventeenth century. How much of the tradition was lost then, like the monastic buildings whose foundations survive as mere shadows in the fields, can only be imagined.

Whilst elements of desert monasticism were preserved in Ireland through the centuries, especially by religious orders within the Roman Catholic Church, the ancient desert monasteries in Egypt and Palestine today probably provide the best example of what the early Irish monasteries were like.

Significance for Christian Churches Today

What significance could these traditions hold for the Church today, as we face the challenges of the new millennium? Coming from our diverse backgrounds and experiences, we can remember and celebrate the fact that the Church was united for the first thousand years of its history, and that the Western Churches shared much in common with the Eastern Churches, until the final schism between East and West in AD 1054. The rediscovery of the connection between the Celtic and the desert traditions has great ecumenical significance, since it reminds us of the deep roots which we all share in the spiritual traditions of the early Church. The monastic remains which lie in our fields remind us that at some deeper level we are all connected to one Christian family, from which all our Churches and traditions have emerged, but which has been broken through centuries of conflict and division.

As we prepare to enter a new millennium, may we find the courage and inspiration to meet the challenges and difficulties facing the Church today; determined, like the saints of old, to seek the paths that lead to renewal and reform; revitalised, as this ancient wisdom from the Bible, the desert and the Celtic tradition speaks powerfully to the Church in our time.

THE CULT OF THE DEAD IN EARLY IRISH (CELTIC) SPIRITUALITY

Seán Ó Duinn

The cult of the dead seems to have been an important part of early Celtic spirituality. The Rule of the *Céli Dé* is quite forthright in this respect:

> There is nothing that a man does on behalf of the soul of one who dies that does not help it, whether vigil or abstinence, or requiem (gabháil n-écnairce) or frequent benediction. Sons ought to do penance for their dead parents. Maedóc of Ferns and all his community spent a full year on bread and water in order to gain the release of the soul of Brandub mac Echach from hell.[1]

This Brandub was King of Leinster and died at the Battle of Slaibre in the year 601/604. Maedóc fought with the demons who were trying to get possession of the king's soul.[2] Obviously, it was a long, drawn-out conflict in which Maedóc and his Community in Ferns were finally successful.

Similarly, in early secular literature, we have the story 'Siabur-Charbat Con Culaind' from the eleventh-century *Leabhar na hUidhre*, in which St Patrick succeeds in getting the great pagan hero Cú Chulainn out of hell for the purpose of persuading King Laoghaire to become a Christian. He succeeds in this and Patrick rewards Cú Chulainn by transferring him from hell to heaven.[3]

Cult of the Dead and Recitation of 'Beati'

A particular connection appears between the cult of the dead and the recitation of the 'Beati' (Psalm 118), called *Biait* in

Irish. This long psalm, with its 22 divisions and 176 verses, seems to have had enormous importance in the lives of clerics and nuns of the early period and had a special efficacy in saving a soul from hell.[4]

Eláir of Loch Cré, now Móin na hInse, near Roscrea, County Tipperary, used to divide the daily recitation of the psalter into three fifties, and recite the Biait and the Magnificat after each fifty psalms *(Gaibtí seom trá teora biádí ocus magnificat la cach nai post p(s)almos biad cech caocad).*[5]

From the opening words *'Beati immaculati in via'*, the psalm (118/119) was associated with a journey, and hence the journey to the Otherworld in death. 'The Biait brings a soul from hell within a year' *(do beir in biat anmain a hiffurn hi cind bliadna)*, it was said, and 'the Biait every day for my soul' *(in biait cech dia ar m'anmainse).*[6]

Both the Milan Glosses and the so-called Psalter of St Caimín of Inis Cealtra on the Shannon[7] connect this psalm with the Babylonian Captivity. The captives finally make their way out of captivity back to Jerusalem. The journey takes one year – 365 days. They travel 176 paces each day and there are 176 verses in the psalm. Interpreted mystically, Babylon corresponds to hell and Jerusalem corresponds to heaven. If the psalm with its 176 verses is recited, then, every day for 365 days on behalf of a dead person, it will bring his soul from hell into heaven.[8]

A story from the Book of Lismore illustrates the power of the Biait:

> Maol Póil Ó Cinnaetha, abbot of the monastery of Cill Becáin had been discussing astrology with another monk. After that, in his sleep, he saw this Gospel Nun who had died six days previously coming towards him complaining bitterly that it didn't matter to him that she

was dead. 'How are things with you there, O Woman?' said he. 'Little you care, indeed,' said she, 'discussing astrology without making intercession for me (*ocus gan m'écnairc-si do ghabháil*). Miserable your performance,' said she. 'What form of intercession do you require from me, O Woman?' said he. 'The Biait, of course,' said she, 'the Biait after the Biait, the Biait above the Biait, the Biait below the Biait,' said she, all in one breath, ordering that the Biait should be said often for her, for nothing except the Mass for the Dead alone is held in greater esteem by God than the Biait.[9]

Colm Cille's Rule

In the Rule attributed to St Colm Cille, the hermit is exhorted to:

> Perform the prayers for the dead with fervour, as if every one of the faithful who died were a special friend of yours.[10]

It does seem that intercession for the dead was a very important and time-consuming element in Celtic monasticism and it may be that the numerous small oratories of the early monasteries were used for this Office of the Dead in somewhat the same fashion as chantries and side-chapels came to be used for Requiem Masses.

Cult of the Dead and Sceilig Mhichíl (Skellig Michael), County Kerry

Perhaps, too, some association with the cult of the dead may be found in one of the most extraordinary monastic sites in the world – that of Skellig Michael (Sceilig Mhichíl). This is a small rocky island off the coast of Kerry, on whose incredibly precipitous and dangerous heights a monastery was founded some time between the sixth and eighth centuries. As well as the recently discovered ruins of a hermitage on the South Peak, clinging precariously to a rock formation 700 feet above the sea, there are six beehive huts and two oratories on the eastern ledge.

The sheer isolation, the exposure to nature in its most elemental forms of rock, wind and sea, the cry of sea-birds, the continual danger, where one false step could plunge a person hundreds of feet into the ocean, create an atmosphere that is at once dramatic and awesome. The stone beehive huts and oratories may have housed an abbot and twelve monks.[11] A small garden forms part of the layout, and the absence of frost on the island may have allowed vegetables to grow in a way hardly to be expected in such an inhospitable setting. Fishing must have been the chief source of food, however, and alternation with the mainland, possible only in good weather, may have been the only means of survival. The deterioration in climate in the thirteenth century may have led to a more complete withdrawal to the mainland monastery of Ballinskelligs, but the island continued to be maintained as a place of pilgrimage.[12]

The Annals of the Four Masters announce for the year 950 '*Bláthmac Sgeillice decc*' (Bláthmac of Skellig dies), but for 1044 it records the death of Aodh of Sccelicc Mhichíl (Aodh of Skellig Michael).[13]

The dedication to St Michael may have taken place between these two dates. Given the predilection for giving rocky heights overlooking the sea to Michael, as at Monte Gargano, Le Mont St Michel, St Michael's Mount, etc., this was only natural, but we may well wonder if the death cult mentioned above had a particular significance for this site.

Tech nDuind – House of Donn (Celtic God of the Dead)

To the south of Skellig Michael is a tiny rocky island called Tech nDuind (the House of Donn). Donn was the god of the dead among the pagan Irish and it was here that the dead assembled: *'Co Tech nDuind frisndailit mairb'* (to Donn's house where the dead assembled – from tenth-century poem). According to Lebor Gabála (Book of Invasions), Donn left as his last bequest: *'Cucum dom thig tissaid uili iar bar n-ésaib'* (To me, to my house, you shall all come after your death).[14]

In Christian tradition, St Michael is the 'Psychopomp', the person who guides the souls of the dead into heaven. We might wonder, then, if the dedication of Skellig to Michael was a direct challenge to Donn, the pagan psychopomp who was engaged in the same kind of operation a few miles to the south. The monastic community would then be involved as associates of Michael in a war against the demons for possession of souls in the very area where the fight was at its fiercest, at Donn's doorstep.

In the eleventh century the cleric and poet Maol Íosa Ó Brolcháin of Armagh addressed St Michael thus:

> *Don amain*
> *tuc cobair, tuc comdídnad*
> *I n-uair techta don talmain.*
>
> *Co daingen*
> *ar chenn m'anama ernaides*
> *tair co n-ilmílib aingel.*[15]

> To my soul,
> give help, give protection
> at the hour of its departure from the world.
>
> Come firmly,
> for my waiting soul,
> come with many thousands of angels.

In the Offertory for the Mass for the Dead, Michael, the standard-bearer, is the one who is to lead the souls of the faithful into the holy light (*'sed signifer sanctus Michael repraesentet eas in lucem sanctam*).

A folklore tradition among the fishermen of that area of Kerry connects Sceilig Mhichíl with Tech nDuind:

> On moonlight nights old fishermen were said to have seen over Skellig Rocks the souls of the dead on their journey to Tír na nÓg – the Otherworld.[16]

Sceilig Pilgrimage – A Rehearsal for the Soul's Journey to Eternity

One of the ancient traditions connected with Sceilig is that of a place of pilgrimage, and the question has been asked if the beehive huts were for pilgrims or for a resident community of monks.[17] At any rate, the pilgrimage involved the most terrifying exercise of squeezing through an opening in the rock called 'The Needle's Eye'. After this, the 'Stone of Pain' and the 'Eagle's Nest' had to be negotiated. A stumble meant a fall on to the projecting rock or into the sea. A long narrow fragment of rock jutting out from the summit over the raging ocean had to be traversed inch by inch. This was known as the 'Spit' or 'Spindle' and led to a stone perched precariously at the end, which the pilgrim kissed. This is probably the stone referred to as the 'Stone of Don' – a possible corruption of Donn. This brings us back again to the alleged connection between Sceilig and Tech nDuind.[18]

This appalling ordeal reaches its climax about 700 feet above the sea, and by making this pilgrimage the devotee believed that he was expediting the journey of his soul to the Otherworld after death.[19] On his way he had to overcome the demons of fear and panic.

There is little doubt but that this pilgrimage was a rehearsal for the soul's journey to eternity and belonged to the same tradition of the Celtic culture as the *eachtra* (adventure) and the *iomramh* (adventure by sea). Only by performing heroic deeds and overcoming seemingly superhuman odds could the hero arrive at the Otherworld and share its spoils, for the gods do not easily part with what belongs to them. The 'Stations' of Sceilig have their analogy in the 'Plain of Ill-Luck', the 'Valley of Monsters', the 'Wild Mountain' and the 'Perilous Bridge', which the hero Cú Chulainn had to traverse before arriving at the Otherworld residence of the female warrior Scáthach, who was to train him in all the feats of battle.[20]

Similarly, the hero Fionn Mac Cumhaill attacks a *Sídh* – a dwelling-place of the supernatural race of the *Tuatha Dé Danann*. His thumb is caught in the door, and when he sucks his thumb on his return to earth, he finds that he is filled with supernatural knowledge, for he has arrived at the very threshold of the Otherworld, where all knowledge resides.[21] Perhaps a similar idea of divine illumination and rehearsal for the Otherworld journey defined the pilgrimage to the monastic sanctuary of Sceilig Mhichíl.

Life was a Quest for the Holy Grail

In the heroic deeds, extraordinary asceticism and individualism of some of the great Celtic monastic figures, a line of continuity may perhaps be discerned with the druidic past, of which Pelagius, with his teaching of absolute confidence in the individual to will and work towards his own salvation, was the heir of the past and the link with the future. The individual had received the *neart* (power), and he could use it, as indeed could be inferred from the Parable of the Ten Talents.[22] Life was a Quest for the Holy Grail.

CELTIC PRAYER

Diarmuid Ó Laoghaire

If Saint Patrick was not the first to write about prayer, he is certainly an important witness in his personal prayer and its quality.

> After I had come to Ireland... I often prayed during the day upwards of a hundred prayers and likewise during the night, even when I was in the woods or on the mountain, I used to pray before the dawn, in spite of snow and frost and rain, nor did that do me any harm, nor was I slothful, for the Spirit was fervent in me at that time. (*Confession*, 16)

> And once again I saw someone praying within me, and I was as it were within my body, and I heard above me, that is above my interior man, and there he prayed strongly and with groans. Meanwhile I was in wonder and confused and I thought who was it that was praying within me, but at the end of the prayer he confirmed, that he was the Spirit. I awoke then and remembered the Apostle saying, the Spirit helps us in our weakness, for we know not what we should ask for. The Spirit pleads for us with inexpressible sighs. (*Confession*, 25)

It should be remembered that Ireland alone of the Celtic countries had not been subject to Roman rule. That is of some significance when we come to talk about Celtic spirituality or prayer. The country was divided into *tuatha* (small kingdoms), each of them ruled by a king.

It is a remarkable fact that within about a century of its inception, the Irish Church had become monastic, not diocesan. True, Patrick had consecrated bishops, but the rural organisation of Ireland into *tuatha* seemed to favour the monastic system, whereby the abbot (who might also be a bishop) wielded jurisdiction. The religious life of the various *tuatha*, ruled by their kings, centred around the monasteries.

Monastic and Scriptural Prayer

We cannot be surprised then if prayer had a monastic flavour and indeed a scriptural flavour. The psalms, as ever, figured largely in the divine office, and we are told in the Lives of the saints, of the young at an early age being put to learn the psalms (in Latin, of course!). In passing, we may mention Bernhard Bischoff, who made a deep study of the scriptural manuscripts on the Continent and found that many of them had been written by Irish monks or their disciples, and could even speak of the mass-production of such manuscripts.[1]

In the *Ancient Irish Litanies*, we have many examples, taken at random, of scriptural prayers:

> 'O corner stone of the Old Testament, O compact of the New Testament, forgive', 'By thy resurrection despoil me of them [sins]'; 'O true physician of every disease and heart-pitier and assister of all misery'; 'I entreat thee, O Holy Jesus by thy four holy evangelists, who wrote thy divine gospels', etc.[2]

It may not be amiss here to give a eulogy of Holy Scriptures found in *Vita Tripartita Sancti Patricii* (The Tri-Partite Life of Saint Patrick), from the fourteenth/fifteenth-century *Leabhar Breac*, which contains much ancient material:

Holy Scripture is one of the gifts of the Holy Spirit by which all ignorance is enlightened and by which all earthly sorrow is dissolved, every spiritual light is illumined, all weakness is strengthened; for it is through Holy Scripture that all heresy and schism is banished from the church, all dissension and disagreement is calmed. In it every grade gets perfect counsel and fitting instruction. Through it all believers in the church banish the stratagems of the devil and vice. For the divine Scripture is mother and gentle nurse, all the believers who consider it and meditate on it are nourished, so that they become through its counsels chosen children of God. For wisdom contributes generously to her children the many flavours of the pleasant-tasting ale, sad the joy of the spiritual food by which they are made ever cheerful and merry.[3]

Contemplative Prayer

Although it is conceded that the Celts were in general a religious people, with a strong sense of presence, which their remains still show, the Christian Celts were considered to be more given to activity than to contemplation. One might use a suasive argument, however, and say that the very quality of the many prayers we possess from those days, in which we see patent love of God, sincerity and earnestness, as well as loving intimacy, could only come as a result of constant contemplation and contact with God.

There are also the 500 examples of the word *díseart* (modern spelling) recorded from around Ireland by Father Edmund Hogan in *Onomasticon Goedelicum*.[4] The placename is clearly from the Latin *desertum*. It is also found in Scotland; and in Wales in the form of *diserth*. These placenames attest to numbers of anchorites in Celtic lands who retired to seek God in prayer.

Saint Columbanus found himself a hermitage in a cave in Annegray, some distance from his monastery at Luxeuil. It is worthwhile quoting, almost at random, a mystical passage from him, while remembering what an evangeliser he was, the father of many monks and monasteries:

> Lord, grant me in the name of Jesus Christ, thy Son, my God, that love which knows no fall so that my lamp may feel the kindling touch and know no quenching, may burn for me and for others may give light. Do thou, Christ, deign to kindle our lamps, Our Saviour most dear to us, that they may shine continually in thy temple, and receive perpetual light from thee the Light Perpetual, so that our darkness may be enlightened and yet the world's darkness may be driven from us....[5]

The importance of meditation is shown in the Life of Saint Íde (Ita). One day a holy nun came to St Íde and said to her:

> 'Tell us in the name of God why you are loved by God more than the other virgins we know of on this earth. For you are fed from above, you heal all diseases by your prayer, you prophecy about things past and future; everywhere you fly from the demons, the angels of God daily speak to you; you continue daily in prayer and in meditation on the Holy Trinity.'

St Íde said to her then:

> 'You yourself have answered your question when you said; "you continue daily without interruption in prayer and in meditation on the Holy Trinity." If anyone acts thus God will always be with him, and if I have been so from

childhood therefore all those things you have mentioned happened to me.' The holy virgin, on hearing the words of the Blessed Íde on prayer, returned rejoicing to her cell.[6]

Crosfhigeall – Body Prayer

Celtic spirituality and prayer have at their centre the Cross. The ancient crosses of Brittany and the medieval calvaries bear silent witness to the fact. *Crosfhigeall,* that is, praying while in a standing position with arms fully extended, was widely performed. Psalm 118, the longest and most popular of the psalms, was often recited while in this posture. The psalm was known in Ireland and Scotland as *Biait* and in Wales as *Bwy.*

There is an Irish tenth-century poem in which the poet calls for the protection of Christ's cross for himself, for every limb, and for wider protection. Here are two verses (in translation):

> The cross of Christ over this face, and thus over my ear.
> The cross of Christ over these eyes, the cross of Christ over this nose.
> The cross of Christ over this mouth, the cross of Christ over this throat.
>
> From the top of my head to the nail of my foot,
> O Christ, against every danger I trust in the protection of thy cross.[7]

The *Lorica* or Breastplate

The above prayer belongs to the class known as *lorica* or breastplate, which was a form of prayer much practised and propagated. The most famous of these and still in use is, doubtless, the *Breastplate of St Patrick*. Here is a shorter but quite universal one, attributed to St Fursa. The Irish has been slightly modernised:

Go raibh cuing reactha Dé ar an ngualainn seo,
Fiosrú an Spioraid Naoimh ar an gceann seo,
Comhartha Chríost ar an éadan seo,
Éisteacht an Spioraid Naoimh sna cluasa seo,
Trí olú an Spioraid Naoimh sa tsróin seo,
Radharc mhuintir neimhe sna súile seo,
Comhrá mhuintir neimhe sa bhéal seo,
Obair Eaglais Dé sna lámha seo,
Leas Dé agus na gcomharsan sna cosa seo,
Go gcónaí Dia sa chroí seo,
Go mba le Dia Athair, an duine seo uile.

May the yoke of the law of God be upon this shoulder,
the coming of the Holy Spirit on this head,
the sign of Christ on this forehead,
the hearing of the Holy Spirit in these ears,
the smelling of the Holy Spirit in this nose,
the vision that the people of heaven have in these eyes,
the speech of the people of heaven in this mouth,
the work of the church of God in these hands,
the good of God and of the neighbour in these feet.
May God dwell in this heart
and this person belong entirely to God the Father.[8]

Completeness

In many traditional folk prayers, the invocation of protection is accompanied by the trait of universality or a desire for completeness. The word *gach* (every) frequently occurs. For instance, a prayer on rising:

An Té a thug saor ón oíche sinn go dtuga sé saor sábhailte
ón lá sinn, le toil Íosa Críost agus na Maighdine Muire, sinn
féin agus a bhfuil againn istigh agus amuigh, thall agus

abhus, i ngach aon áit ina bhfuil siad. Tabhair saor sábháilte sinn féin agus a bhfuil againn idir dhuine agus bheithíoch.

Iarraim ar Dhia agus ar an Maighdean Muire, sinn féin agus ár leanaí go léir agus gach aon atá ag dul ar strae a chur ar a leas agus ar staid na ngrást agus ar shlí na fírinne, i ngrá Dé agus na gcomharsan.

May he who brought us safely through the night bring us safe and sound through the day, Jesus Christ and the Virgin Mary willing, all we have, indoors and outdoors, far and near, in every place where they are. Bring us safe and sound, both people and animals.

I ask God and the Virgin Mary to bring ourselves and all our children safe and sound and to put all who are going astray on the right road and in the state of grace and on the way of truth, in the love of God and of the neighbours.[9]

Breton Prayers

There was much coming and going between the Celtic countries, so we cannot be surprised if they borrowed from one another in terms of prayers. We have Breton prayers similar to those found in Ireland and Scotland:

En anv Doue d'amgwele ez an,
An tri ael mat a saludan.
Daou em c'halon, un all em penn,
Jesus ha Mari em c'hrec'henn.
A pedan da zont d'm zifenn,
Em dihun hag em c'housket.

In the name of God to my bed I go,
The three good angels I salute.
Two in my heart, another in my head,
Jesus and Mary in my breast.
I pray them to come to protect me,
In my waking and in my sleeping.

Va ael mat, kannad Doue,
Mirit va c'horf ha va ene;
Va mirit diouzh an droukspered
Ha dreist pep tra holl diouzh ar pec'hed
Me ho ped, sent ha santezed,
Ma vin ganeoch gwarezet;
Grit din-me kaout digant Jezuz
Ur marv mat hag evurus.

My good angel, messenger of God,
Protect my body and my soul;
Protect me from the evil spirit
And above all else, from sin.
I pray you, saints, men and women
To protect me;
Obtain for me from Jesus
A good and happy death.[10]

God or Christ as *Rí* (King)

We referred earlier to the organisation of rural Ireland into
tuatha (small kingdoms). When God or Christ was addressed as
Rí (King), as he often was and still is, it being ever the favourite
term for God and Christ, remote majesty is not implied but
rather the respect and familiarity due to one who could be
related in kinship to many in the small kingdom.

The same term occurs in Scottish Gaelic, although the spelling may differ (*Rígh*). We may be familiar with an expression such as *A Rí na Glóire* (O King of Glory), but in Tír Chonaill (County Donegal), we may hear simply *An Rí* (the King) – '*Go ndéana An Rí a mhaith dó*' (May God be good to him).

A very special term, *Rí an Domhnaigh* (the King of Sunday), also occurs in Ireland and Scotland. In a fifteenth-century Irish poem we read '*Rí an Domhnaigh mo Dhochtúirse*' (O King of Sunday, my Physician). And in Scotland we find verses such as: '*Chan 'eil ar muir no ar fonn na bheir air Righ an Domhnaigh*' (There is not in sea or on land that can overcome the King of Sunday).

'Muire' (Our Lady)

As regards Our Lady, the discovery by Professor Carney of the poems to Our Lady by the mid-eighth-century poet Bláthmac has shown us a mature devotion and compassion for Mary and her suffering Son which anticipated by half a millennium the writings of St Bernard. In one poem, the poet speaks with a remarkable intimacy to Mary. Here, in translation, is a short extract:

> Come to me loving Mary
> that I may keen with you your very dear one.
> Alas that your son to the cross should go,
> he a great diadem, a beautiful hero.[11]

We know that 'Muire' in the course of time became the sole name for Our Lady in Ireland. 'Mac Muire' (Son of Mary), probably from the Welsh 'Mab Mair', was also used as a respectful yet familiar appellation for Jesus Christ at a time when the wider Church tended to emphasise his transcendent divinity.

The Rosary of Our Lady became very popular in Ireland because in Penal days it took the place of the proscribed Mass. It gradually found its way into everyday idiom. This is how one person described the effect that fervent recital of the communal Rosary could have:

> *Focail bhreatha bheannaithe a bhíodh acu iontu agus dhéanaidís aithris leis an bhfíorumhlaíocht cheart, d'ardaídís iad féin agus na daoine a bhíodh ag éisteacht leo idir chorp agus anam suas go doirse na bhFlaitheas.*

> They were truly holy words for them who gave them out with humility, so that it brought them and those who listened to them to the very gates of heaven.[12]

Conclusion

We have described some of the central elements in Celtic prayer. We began with an example of St Patrick's fervency and we conclude as we enter the next millennium with a recollection of devotion among our ancestors, as described by an anonymous visitor to Ireland during the dark and turbulent years of the 1590s:

> They rise at midnight to pray and meditate, at which some spend a full hour, others half an hour. They always light the fire at that time.[13]

CELTIC MYTHS IN HEALING PROCESS
A JOURNEY (WITH CÚ CHULAINN) TO THE WARRIOR OF HEART

Kate Fitzpatrick

Introduction

This essay explores the way in which myths can be used in the healing process. I find that all of the old Irish myths are relevant to our psychology today. The Warrior of Heart is a journey of archetypal soul-making that came from my inner work with the story of *Cú Chulainn*, the warrior champion of the Ulster Mythic Cycle.

In our society we need healing, both personally and collectively. I believe that this needs to come from a deep place within us, and for therapeutic work to be effective, it must encompass a healing of the soul.

Myths are the language of the soul. They are the stories that are connected to the soul's journey through life and the challenges of being human. When we work with myth in the healing process, we are re-weaving the original myths. We are restoring the balance of our soul's need for myth and our need to be in balance with nature. With the healing symbols that we create in myth-making, we are dreaming the future into manifest existence.

Myth in Personal Process

The making of myth arises from the presence of archetypes in the rich depth of the psyche. The energy of the archetypes colours our daily lives in a mysterious and unfathomable way, manifesting in images. Everyday events, such as birth, death, marriage, family, the eternal rhythms of being human, have archetypal roots. It is by using these archetypes, along with the backdrop of the seasons, the winds, weather and landscape, that we create mythology.

We imbue these stories with emotions. Myths contain within them the great dilemmas and conflicts that are an eternal part of life. Influenced by the numinosity of the archetypal roots, we create our myths in larger-than-life characters and dramas.

It is the soul's desire to create myths. I can use the myth like a vessel that holds my pain, my feelings, my joy. Each image I create adds to the whole story and my personal biography will come to life and resonate in the story I choose to work with. This is an alchemical process, and not only will I be transformed but the myth itself will evolve and transform in the collective unconscious. How exactly this happens is a mystery. It is in the realm of the sacred and in the unknowable nature of archetypes. This is the process of *soul-making.*

Irish Mythology and the Archetype of War

Mythologies from each culture reflect the nature of the people who create them. It is interesting that for all the beauty and resonance of our Celtic myths, they are predominantly about war. Why, I wonder, has the archetype of war predominated in the Irish psyche to such an extent? The whole mythic history of Ireland is concerned with wars and battles to defend the shores and boundaries of the land. The glorification of war is still part of our mythic expression. Using songs and ballads, we have imbued every battle in the past 800 years with a numinous hue and larger-than-life passion. What is this obsession with war in our culture and what has been the mythic function of this for us?

Archetype of the Warrior – Cú Chulainn

The archetype of the warrior is connected to the archetype of war. This constellation is activated when stability is threatened by an outside force that is invasive or destructive. It is a matter of defending boundaries and standing up to the invader.

In personal psychology, the ego will defend itself when threatened, and so there is an equivalent experience in society that draws on this archetype to defend the ego boundaries. We know it as an energy that is active and *yang*, confrontational or defensive.

Cú Chulainn was the archetypal warrior champion in Irish mythology. So let us take a closer look at the factors that set the scene for his life and trace the connections between his story and the inner journey that I call the Warrior of Heart.

Background to the Cú Chulainn Story

In the Bronze Age, from 3,000 BC to the time of Christ, a patriarchal, male-dominated ethos was spreading through all of the ancient goddess-based civilisations. This culture was based on the glorification of the sun-god, who rose to power through war and conquest.[1] To what extent the Celts were patriarchal is not clear, and when and through what influences they became patriarchal is not recorded directly in the literature. They were related to the Indo-Europeans and yet they also have their origins back in matriarchal-based neolithic cultures.

The deities of the older Celtic myths, therefore, are centred in the goddess-based culture. These deities are known as the *Tuatha Dé Danann*. They are the divine race of the goddess and their natures reflect a duality and balance of male and female. There are male gods with plenty of *yin*, the feminine principle, and many goddesses with *yang*, the masculine principle, in their characters. These myths are based on right relationship to the sacred land.

In the later myths, however, such as those relating to Cú Chulainn, the patriarchal archetypes of war and the warrior come to dominate.

Macha's Curse

The story of *Macha* leaves us in no doubt that Conchobhar Mac Neasa's Ulster had inculcated the patriarchal glorification of the cult of the warrior as the supreme code of existence. This woman Macha, who was the Celtic horse-goddess, and just about to give birth, was forced to run a race for public spectacle against the horses of the king.[2] As horse-goddess, she represents fertility and the untamed power of a woman connected to the natural mysteries of her body. She cursed the men of Ulster for this violation.

And so begins a cycle in Ulster where women were used for sport, where pregnant women were no longer sacred, where the name of Macha could not be spoken, and where men have been cursed by the goddess.

Into this culture the hero who became known as Cú Chulainn was born. His mother was *Dectera*, a sister of the king. His father was *Lugh*, of the divine race of the Tuatha Dé Danann. And the boy, named originally as *Setanta*, was part-human and part-divine. His Dé Danann birthright sets him apart and free of Macha's curse. What kind of a hero's mission did he come into the world to achieve?

Cú Chulainn's Role in the Ulster Myths

Cú Chulainn is depicted as a warrior of phenomenal physical stamina. He is trained by *Scáthach*, a woman warrior on the Isle of Skye,[3] in what seems to be the tradition of the Indo-European warrior cult.[4] This training involves the ability of the warrior to shape-shift on the battlefield and manifest the transpersonal power of a wild animal. In Cú Chulainn, this shape-shifting is described as *Raistradh* or battle frenzy.[5]

The main story about Cú Chulainn is the fight with *Meadhbh* in the famous story, the *Táin Bó Cuailgne* (the Battle of the Bulls).[6] Meadhbh is the archetype of the fierce Celtic warrior queen. She represents the Old Celtic matriarchal order that predominated in Ireland at that time. She is able to call on men from all of the other provinces to issue her assault on the Ulster warriors.

The story of the *Táin* tells of this battle, fought between the old regime in the rest of Ireland and the new order in Ulster. The Bulls represent the power and potency of *yang* energy. Which is stronger and bigger? The White Bull of Connaught representing the matriarchal *yang* of the old goddess civilisations, or the Brown Bull of Cooley, representing the spread of the Indo-European solar deity[7] and the influx of patriarchal civilisation.

Cú Chulainn, who becomes champion warrior to the king, has a crucial role in this battle. When the rest of the Ulster warriors are struck down by Macha's curse, he fights Meadhbh's men singlehandedly. It is the saga of these battles that Cú Chulainn is famous for. They form the core of the Ulster Mythic Cycle.

Cú Chulainn and his Inner Divine Feminine

There is another piece to Cú Chulainn's destiny. Why are there so many of the feminine archetypes impinging on his life? We have already mentioned Scáthach. *Emer* is his wife. She is very much a match for him, and despite his numerous infidelities, he always returns to her. There is also the *Morríghan*, goddess of war. What does she want when she approaches him so frequently during his battles, and yet he continues to spurn her? And if Macha's humiliation represents an exile, not only of the power of women from Ulster but of the Tuatha Dé Danann as the divine race, is Cú Chulainn's role to restore this balance in some way?

Questions such as these drew me to explore an episode in the *Táin* which describes Cú Chulainn's call to the Otherworld. The text tells us:

Cú Chulainn as he lay asleep after hunting had a vision of two Dé Danann women who came to him and beat him till he was all but dead and could not lift a hand to defend himself. He lay in sore sickness for a year.[8]

In psychological terms, this beating by the Dé Danann women symbolises the death of the old ego. Cú Chulainn can no longer draw on his warrior skills to deal with this episode. The great champion is beaten down by two women of a divine race. This surely represents a battle of a different kind – a spiritual battle.

Cú Chulainn then receives the call to individuate and become whole. Here the goddess *Fand*, also of the Tuatha Dé Danann, symbolises his inner divine feminine and his call to integration:

Then a man came and told him to go back to the pillar. He found a woman in a green mantle who told him that Fand, the Pearl of Beauty, wife of *Manannán Mac Lir*, the Sea God had set her love on him and she wanted his help to fight demons Manannán had put in her realm. The price of his help would be the love of Fand.[9]

Initially Cú Chulainn does not respond, but eventually, since the call does not go away, he decides to investigate further:

Laeg his charioteer is sent to the Otherworld by Cú Chulainn to report upon Fand. He came home with a report of Fand's surpassing beauty and Cú Chulainn then betook himself thither. He had a battle in the dense mist with the demon, then he abode with Fand enjoying all the delights of fairyland for a month, after which he bade her farewell and appointed a trysting place on earth, the Strand of the Yew tree, where she was to meet him.[10]

Cú Chulainn is not prepared for the effects that Fand has on him. He is softened and changed through his experience of love for her; a whole new part of him is awakened, a part not experienced through his warrior training. From a psychological point of view, Cú Chulainn's challenge is to integrate this experience of the feminine with his everyday life.

But this does not happen with tragic and far-reaching consequences. The story continues:

> Emer, Cú Chulainn's wife, hears of the tryst and comes with fifty women armed with knives to slay Fand.

Fand, however, has no intention of taking Cú Chulainn from Emer. She tells Emer 'it is I who must go'. Emer is surprised by Fand's honesty, and her need to fight melts away in the face of the power of love of this Dé Danann woman.

Manannán Mac Lir then comes to support Fand. He asks her:

> 'Wilt Thou return to me or abide with Cú Chulainn?'

She answers:

> 'In truth, I will go with thee, Manannán.'

So Fand went with Manannán, and he, the great sea god:

> shook his cloak between Cú Chulainn and Fand so that they might meet no more throughout eternity.[11]

Cú Chulainn's Melancholy

Manannán sets the boundary between the human and the divine. Emer never gets back the Cú Chulainn she once knew. Cú Chulainn's experience with Fand turns his secure identity as Ulster's Warrior Champion inside out. He remains for a long time in a melancholic reverie, refusing food and drink. He is unable to put a boundary between the human and the divine, and so remains lost in the mists and illusions of the Otherworld.

In psychological terms we would say that Cú Chulainn is unable to hold the 'tension of opposites', that is, of his experience of love for both of these women – Emer the human woman, his wife, a representation of his outer human self, and Fand, the divine woman, a manifestation of his inner divine feminine.

The Drink of Forgetfulness – Negation of the Whole Experience

Emer persuades a druid to give Cú Chulainn a drink of forgetfulness in the hope that it will cure him. Alas, this is the negation of the whole experience. It puts Cú Chulainn back into unconsciousness; he eventually goes insane and is pursued by Meadhbh until his death.

The drink of forgetfulness represses all the energy of transformation that is necessary to transcend the tension of opposites and integrate the experience of the divine feminine into daily life. With the feminine integrated into consciousness, we could have seen a man of great maturity and courage emerge, who might have mediated the challenges presented by the patriarchal invasion in the world.

Patriarchy Continues: A Pivotal Point in the Irish Psyche

Cú Chulainn's failure to integrate the experience of the divine feminine into his warrior identity guarantees that patriarchy continues to dominate. Cú Chulainn becomes a victim in a whole system that he has spent his life defending. The chance to redeem Macha's curse is lost.

I suggest this is a pivotal point in the relationship between the human and the divine in the evolution of the Irish psyche. The power of the natural duality, symbolised in the Tuatha Dé Danann, goes further underground, and the archetype of the victim takes root in the collective unconscious.

Soul-Making and Transformations

Now, how does this story of Cú Chulainn point the way to a Warrior of Heart? There are four main threads of soul-making that I have woven with this myth. The first part is the transformation of the victim into a warrior. The second part is the reintegration of the damaged 'feeling' function. Thirdly, there is the transformation of the patriarchal masculine at the archetypal core. The final piece is the integration of all of this in the alchemy that creates a Warrior of Heart.

1) The Transformation of Victim to Warrior

This is done primarily in the body. The victim is the abused part of us and it manifests in our lack of ability to stand up and fight when we are threatened. The body is cut off from its source of power. In transforming this victim place, it is necessary to release pain and rage from the body in order to restore the natural instinctive power to defend ourselves in danger. Without this transformation, the intention behind any fight or war is to destroy. The unconscious rage, pain and desire for revenge is still motivating the action.

In the Eastern martial arts, *Yin* and *Yang* work together to conserve energy and ultimately to conserve life. This is the balance aimed for in the body of the transformed victim.

2) The Integration of the Feeling Function

In Jungian psychology, the feeling function is associated with the feminine. The damaged feeling function may appear in dreams of men and women as a little girl or a woman who is frightened, crying and in hiding. The governing principle of the feeling function is relationship. It is the ability to 'think' with the heart, to feel for the other, and a desire not to destroy.

The work of healing the damaged feeling function is restoring the balance of *yin* in our hearts and souls. In the Cú Chulainn story, it is Fand who holds the archetypal image of *yin*. She is connecting Cú Chulainn back to his soul, while Emer connects him to human love.

The transformation of the feeling function is done in relationship to others. The outcome is that there is no need to destroy or invade the body or soul of another being. The ego is secure and there is an ability to be in right relationship, not just with people, but with all of nature.

The Indo-European warrior cult, in which Cú Chulainn was trained, was abusive to the transpersonal powers of nature. It strengthened warriors to dominate and destroy. This was the beginning of the war ethos that has dominated the patriarchal era and has given us a model of the masculine principle that is invasive and does not honour boundaries. It is ego-based and not in connection with the greater whole. It is time now to allow a different kind of masculine to evolve.

3) The transformation of the Inner Masculine at the Archetypal Core

The work of transforming the inner masculine is a work of soul. It is the weaving of images and emotion that ultimately change the archetypal core. In the Cú Chulainn story, Manannán Mac Lir, the sea-god, models a masculine energy that is able to set good boundaries and to be a 'man of the heart'. He holds the balance of *yin* and *yang* of the Tuatha Dé Danann. It is a masculine principle that holds power and authority without being abusive. In mythology, Manannán is associated with the holding of the boundaries of the land of Ireland.[12]

The work of healing the inner masculine is not done separately from the body work or the healing of the feeling function, but simultaneously. The stages of transformation are not rigid. The pattern of healing in the psyche is a spiral one. Over a period of years, the weaving of each part is done and re-done until it finally holds as a permanent change in the psyche.

4) The Emergence of the Warrior of the Heart

At this stage the Warrior of Heart begins to emerge. This warrior is motivated, not from insecurity or fear of invasion, but from an awareness of the inter-connectedness of life. It is the paradox of the ability to take a stand, whilst still holding the intention of love in the heart. It is a connection to the deeper archetypal love that bathes the universe in grace. This love re-weaves the fragmented parts of us and re-connects us to nature. It is the Heart in its greatest sense as a symbol of wholeness.

Relevance of Cú Chulainn's Challenge today

If myths are part of the psychological history of a nation, then unfinished business still lies repressed in the Irish psyche. The initiation that Cú Chulainn failed in, is still needed in both men and women here. It is an inner battle – to restore the balance of masculine and feminine and heal the damaged soul. The goddess needs to be returned to Ulster. The heart is still in exile. Not the sentimental heart that sings the grief of ages, but the balanced, receptive heart that is connected to the inner soul and is tough enough to stand up and take its place in the outer world.

In everyday life, the Warrior of Heart is not about being at war. Rather, it is a balance of *yin* and *yang* energy within the heart of an individual or a nation, such that war is no longer necessary. It is about having clear boundaries, yet remaining open to outsiders. From this secure place can be communicated that invasions will not be tolerated.

The stability of *yin* and *yang* makes us less vulnerable to either personal invasion that destroys the feminine in spirit or the collective invasions that have oppressed us and fragmented the Soul of this land since earliest times. As a nation, we can heal these old wounds, release the pain of ages of oppression and walk forward to a place of new birth – no longer investing our ego identity in the role of invaded and colonised victim.

With the Warrior of Heart strong in our national psyche and the goddess Macha restored to her rightful place, we could create a society where death is not conquered by death, which is the code of the war machine of patriarchy. If the mysteries of transformation are respected and honoured, then physical death is not a necessary sacrifice for change.

This is the mystery at the root of the archetype of the Morríghan, who appears repeatedly to Cú Chulainn in the *Táin* (and who is famously depicted on the statue in the GPO, Dublin, as the crow perched on his shoulder). As goddess of transformation, the Morríghan comes into her full power, pointing relentlessly to the shadow both within and without, demanding that it be faced.

We do have to let go of what no longer serves. This is *the death* that is demanded: old ego attitudes have to go. On a collective level, old cultural attitudes that have fed the insecure egos of nations have to die so that new cultures of balance, integration and diversity can be reborn.

CELTIC RESOURCES
FOR A PEACE PROCESS

Johnston McMaster

In the early 1970s I began to discover the story of the Celtic Christian tradition, and realised I was discovering something which, in a strange way, I felt I had always known. There seemed to be familiar roots, though I had not been told the story before. That I felt it was part of me is, perhaps, not surprising, because my mother was only third generation removed from Cornwall, where the Celtic tradition was strong. My father's side of the family provided a strong Scottish connection, which was also coming out of Celtic roots.

Two Methodist Church appointments in Cork and Wicklow, located me close to historical Celtic sites of beauty. The appreciation of the Celtic sense of place and presence grew and the spiritual quest was enriched by visits to Gúgán Barra and Glendalough. Now I find myself teaching courses, leading retreats, workshops and seminars on Celtic spirituality and dealing in my work with Irish history, politics and cultural traditions and theology.

Returning to Northern Ireland: Realising the Need for an Applied Spirituality

Returning to Northern Ireland in 1980 meant taking seriously the core issues dividing the community and the development of an approach to community relations, ecumenism, reconciliation and community building. All of this has required theological reflection and spirituality to be concrete and contextualised. Theological and spiritual vision always translate into social and political relationships. There is no theology or spirituality that is politically neutral. This does not mean a politicised theology or spirituality, which usually becomes a destructive form of religious nationalism, the orange and green shades that have plagued Ireland. It is about theology and spirituality in the public place. Celtic spirituality, past or present, is no exception. In its earliest form it always had a public context and the present cannot be any different.

Unless my involvement with Celtic spirituality is simply historical, or worse, romanticised, then it needs to translate into the contemporary context, which is a long-term peace process involving attitudinal, behavioural and structural transformation. A spirituality for the long haul is needed, which means exploring, developing and practising an applied spirituality. This has motivated an approach to Celtic spirituality as a potential bridge and shared heritage between Protestant and Catholic. There is a potential for reconciliation within the common heritage so long as it is developed as contextualised or applied Celtic spirituality.

The Context

Essential to the peace process in Northern Ireland is the creation of a meaningful civil society. Civil society is essentially about two things. It is about creating and preserving relationships and enabling communication in the widest sense. Civil society is not concerned with acquiring power or about political competition or rivalry. It is about promoting meaningful and quality relationships based on equality, reciprocity and trust. At the heart of civil society, therefore, are relationships and communication. Without these, politics has no legitimacy or effectiveness. No political settlement will work effectively in Northern Ireland unless we have a meaningful civil society. That is the precondition and prerequisite.

Building relationships and opening up channels of communication are key roles for Churches in Northern Ireland.

And relationships and communication mean relationships and communication between Catholics and Protestants and all who do not or no longer identify with those categories. To engage with such a primary role is to move beyond the prisons of our confessionalism and dogma; beyond our preoccupation with purity of theological or doctrinal identity to a way of being Church that is more relational, that is more authentically biblical and creatively theological. It is out of this primary relational model of spirituality, reading Scripture, doing theology and being Church that the Christian community has its greatest role in the present and future of Northern Ireland. But religious divisions are part of the problem in Northern society and politics. There is a Protestant-Catholic divide, which is not only political and cultural, but also religious.

An Underground Stream Belonging to Irish Gael and Scottish Planter

There is, however, a faith expression and spirituality older than the historical events that divide us. Behind the political dynamics and particular historical experiences of the twelfth, sixteenth and seventeenth centuries, there is an older and deeper tradition. It is the Celtic tradition, a deep, more often underground stream, that belongs to the Irish Gael and Scottish Planter. It is the earliest and indigenous expression of faith and spirituality of our two islands. It is an older tradition in which Irish Catholics and Protestants could find a bridge or common meeting-place. Celtic Christian spirituality has deep insights, which can resource the building of a just and peaceful future. There are Celtic resources for a peace process that will require not months, but decades. A just political settlement, to be built on and sustained, needs a truly civil society, where relationships and communication are of primary importance. In turn, these require foundations that are spiritual and ethical. Celtic spirituality can provide common resources from a common source. Some of the common resources are:

1. The Trinity As Community in the Celtic Christian Tradition

At the heart of Celtic spirituality is the vision and experience of God as Trinity. The pre-Christian focus on triads and trinities gave Celtic people a natural inclination towards a Trinitarian experience. When the Christian story entered Celtic society and consciousness, Trinity was already a familiar idea. Experience, thought and imagination naturally embraced the Trinitarian vision of God. A classic expression of Celtic Christian spirituality is the poem traditionally known as *St Patrick's Breastplate*. The poem, which is probably eighth-century, and therefore much later than Patrick himself, is centred on the Trinity. 'I bind unto myself today the strong name of the Trinity.' The style of poem or prayer is known as a *lorica*, a kind of protection prayer. It may well have been a morning dressing prayer. For all the day's experiences, journeys and relationships, the Trinity was invoked.

The *Confession* document, considered to be authentically Patrick, is also deeply rooted in the Trinity. Patrick's profession of faith is built around a Trinitarian framework. Celtic spirituality is essentially Trinitarian.

Uniting the Mystical and the Practical

At the heart of the Celtic approach to reality was the ability to hold together the deeply mystical and the profoundly practical. The mystical and the practical were two sides of the one coin. This is true in the Celtic approach to the Trinity.

Much of our traditional Western theology has often approached the Trinity as a philosophical and speculative problem. At a more popular level, the Trinity is perceived as being a mathematical conundrum to be solved. For the mystical and practical Celt, the Trinity was an experience to be lived.

Celtic theology and spirituality have more kinship with the theology and spirituality of the East than the West. The Eastern Cappadocian theologians envisioned and experienced the Trinity more as a community and relational. At the heart of the godhead are relationships. God is social being and envisioned as a community of harmonious relationships. Trinity is the divine community centred in self-giving love.

Within the Trinity, there is also the experience of differentiated union. In this vision of God there is real diversity in unity and unity in diversity. The three-one God is a community of mutuality, equality and reciprocity. Trinity is the divine community of interacting, interconnected and interdependent relationships.

The Eastern theologians used a particular word to give creative and rich expression to their vision of God. It was *perichoresi,* expressing the interpenetration and interactive nature of the divine community. The metaphor is even more dynamic and creative because it expresses the image of dance. The dance of the Trinity is the daring vision of God. To be baptised into the life of the Trinity or to bind to oneself the strong name of the Trinity, is to enter into the creative movement and dance of the divine community. It is this rich, creative vision of God that is at the heart of Celtic spirituality.

A Model for Community Relationships

In the holism of the mystical and practical, the Trinity is also the model of community. The mystical vision of God becomes the model for community relationships. This has concrete implications when applied to the challenge and struggle to build real community in Northern Ireland. The Celtic vision of God critiques and challenges all our separatism, isolationism, sectarian division, and its exclusion and excluding zones. It challenges the sectarian dehumanising of each other, the demonisation of one another and our respective communities and identities. It calls us beyond ideas of benign apartheid or coexistence. It provides a model of community in which diversity is necessary, acceptable, welcome, and even to be celebrated. Differences need not be feared, become threatening or result in cultural, political or religious dominance. Diversity in unity and unity in diversity, mutuality, equality, interdependence and interrelationships, are ultimate realities because they are of the very essence of God, who is Trinity.

Trinity also models community as dynamic and creative dance in which all count in the movement and music of rich diversity and harmony. We step out together.

The vision and experience of God as Trinity at the heart of Celtic spirituality provides a vision and experience of community. Trinity can inspire and shape the task of building new community and relationships within the peace process.

2. The Primacy of the Relational in the Celtic Christian Tradition

What mattered most to early Celtic Christians were relationships. Faith, life and spirituality were primarily relational. If the Celtic vision of God and faith experience did not translate into relationships at personal and community levels, then serious question marks needed to be raised.

Celtic Christians were not primarily concerned with dogmas and doctrines. Faith for them was not a set of propositions nor a system of theology. Indeed they were very untidy about definitions and doctrines. Neither was it about ideologies and principles.

For over four hundred years Irish Churches have defined themselves in opposition to each other. We have often been preoccupied with preserving the purity of our dogmas, doctrines and theological systems. We work out of a confessional mind-set. Purity of confession is more important than relationships.

In politics we have created ideologies, sectarian ideologies and exclusive ideologies, which have often used God to give them legitimacy. Principles are set in stone, and sticking uncompromisingly to one's principles, be they principles of faith or politics, or both merged together, has become a cardinal virtue. Needless to say, all of this leaves little room or none at all for tolerance, negotiation, relationships and communication.

Relationship Over Dogma

Celtic spirituality offers another way. What matters more than dogmas, ideologies and principles are relationships. Dogmas, doctrines, ideologies and principles are too often destructive of relationships, block communication and undermine community, certainly inclusive community.

Celtic spirituality is primarily relational. The vision and experience of God translates into the vision and praxis of inclusive and diverse relationships and shared community. The Celtic relational insight can resource our implementation of a just settlement and the building of a peaceful and inclusive community.

3. The Practice of Hospitality in the Celtic Christian Tradition

Celtic spirituality was and is communitarian. The distinctive model of Church that emerged in Ireland was that of the monastic community. Unlike much later monastic development, these Celtic monastic communities were open. They were open to all. They were places of hospitality, where the poor and suffering were welcomed. They were places of refuge, where safety was guaranteed. One of the great Irish communities was at Kildare, founded by Brigid. It became known as the City of the Poor, such was its reputation for hospitality, compassion and generosity. These were inclusive communities, where the stranger was welcomed and embraced. The practice of hospitality was at the heart of Celtic spirituality.

The Demonisation of 'the Other' in Northern Ireland

In Northern Ireland, communities have often been defined in terms of exclusion. The other is demonised; a threat to identity and therefore to political future. Relational boundaries must be maintained and societal structures created to ensure a form of apartheid, from segregated schools to job discrimination. Communication is either not encouraged or avoided by a form of politeness in which religion, politics, culture and history are never spoken about. Socially, culturally, religiously and educationally, we create and maintain our exclusion zones.

Some feel that all we can hope for is a kind of benign apartheid or coexistence, a kind of cold peace. Yet we need to face our crunch issues and build some form of authentic community. For a just political settlement to work, change is required.

Openness to 'the Other' in the Celtic Tradition

Celtic spirituality with its practice of hospitality can open us up to one another. It draws us to the practice of inclusion, in which there is openness and generosity of spirit. It offers us the possibility of embrace, especially of the stranger, which many of us are to each other. It can inspire the gesture of compassion and the gesture of reconciliation. It may even lead us to the embrace of the enemy and the many victims of our troubles, including the perpetrators, who are also victims.

The Celtic practice of hospitality today is essentially about justice. It is about justice as just relationships, where the others' sacredness is affirmed, their experience is entered into and their story is really heard. It is also about just relations socially, economically and politically. Our situation now cries out for gestures of compassion, justice and reconciliation. The Celtic practice of hospitality offers a radical resource for the building of a new future.

4. The Art of Penitence in the Celtic Christian Tradition

The Celtic Church produced a whole range of Penitentials. These were penitential manuals providing a confessor, or soul friend, as the person was known in the Celtic tradition, with pastoral guidance for spiritual healing and direction. The Penitentials dealt with the human reality of sin and its effects.[1]

Like everything else, the Penitentials were contextualised. They emerged from a particular culture at a particular time. In their detail they are not timeless. The rigor with which penance was sometimes applied may be a turn-off to late-twentieth-century people. Yet, there are important insights, with much to say to our implementation of a just and a peaceful settlement.

In the Celtic art of penitence, sin was not understood as the breaking of laws or disobedience against a divine law-giver, still less a divine law-enforcement officer. With that key insight that everything is ultimately relational, sin was essentially about broken relationships. It was a moral disease that required healing; not even about individual acts, but a condition, a disease that produced dis-eased relationships. So the Celtic Christians spoke of healing or cure in relation to sin.

Personal, Relational and Societal Healing/Penitence

Columbanus, the great sixth-century Irish Celtic saint, underlined two aspects of the art of penitence. One was doing penance, which had to do with deep personal healing. The

101

other was 'making satisfaction', especially satisfaction to the victim. Here again, the primacy of the relational was being underlined. Making satisfaction was about undoing the social effects of sin and taking seriously the social dimension of reconciliation.

With our over-emphasised culture of individualism, not only have relationships been undermined or dis-eased, our views of sin, forgiveness and reconciliation have only paid attention to the vertical dimension. It is just me and God, which has led to a very cheap idea of grace. We have disconnected the horizontal from the vertical and therefore ignored the relational reality of sin, as well as reconciliation. As long as we stick with the vertical dimension, we avoid the social effects of sin and the social dimensions of reconciliation. We do not then deal with the structural reality of sin, nor are we open to the possibility of structural transformation and reconciliation. From the Celtic perspective on penitence, we are challenged to face the need and possibility for personal, relational and societal healing. The Celtic art of penitence is about the healing of relationships.

Truth, Justice and Reconciliation in Northern Ireland

Making satisfaction, especially to the victim, is particularly pertinent and painful in the Northern Ireland situation. Can there really be forgiveness and reconciliation without truth and justice? Perhaps in Northern Ireland we too will need some kind of truth and reconciliation commission. There are deep hurts to be dealt with, and if they are not healed, they will be inherited by the next generation. They already impinge on the hearts and minds, attitudes and feelings of the young. And no section of the community has a monopoly on suffering; as well as victims, there are prisoners who are also victims of our diseased history and relationships. In what ways can we make satisfaction, practice the art of penitence, which can undo the social effects of sin and liberate each other and each other's community from our diseased pasts into social realities of reconciliation?

We may well need to recover this Celtic art of penitence as we seek for the healing of our community and the construction of a just and peaceful future for ourselves and for our children's children, even, as the Amerindians say, 'to the seventh generation'.

Celtic Statecraft and the Importance of the 'King's Truth'

Celtic statecraft (deserving of more substantial treatment than what follows) encompasses a simple but profound insight derived from the role of the king. Utterly important was the 'King's truth'. Celtic literature and law expressed it in this way:

> If the king is just, his reign will be peaceful and prosperous;
> If he is guilty of injustice, the natural elements will rise up against him.[2]

It is a profound political insight which is also profoundly spiritual and ethical. Peace comes with justice. Injustice goes against the very moral grain of the universe. An inseparable link is made between truth, justice and peace. Without these, the new political, communal and relational future will not be achieved. With the best opportunity for centuries to build a new future, our common Celtic heritage offers a spirituality of politics or a political spirituality. It offers a vision of God and community for our future.

CREATIVE WORSHIP
IN THE CELTIC TRADITION

Dara Molloy

Creative worship means using one's imagination and creativity. It means personal empowerment – using our own ability to create meaningful worship rather than relying on others to do it for us. It means being able to use material from within a tradition without being limited or constrained by it.

The Irish (Celtic) Spiritual Tradition

For our purposes, the Celtic spiritual tradition can be divided into two periods. The first period is the pre-Christian Celtic tradition, what I call the Irish Old Testament. This spans 5,000 years and has given us such spiritual riches as the tumuli at Newgrange, Knowth and Dowth, the festival of *Samhain* (Halloween), the *turas deiseal* or rounds of the holy well, a pantheon of gods and goddesses, and a great collection of stories.

The second period is the Celtic Christian one, which began at the time of Saint Patrick and came to its apex in Ireland from the seventh to the tenth centuries, and was eventually superseded by the Roman tradition from the twelfth century onwards.

In this tradition there are numerous resources for worship. The primary resources are story, landscape and culture.

Story as a Resource for Worship

The Pre-Christian Irish Tradition

There are different cycles within the pre-Christian Irish tradition, from which stories can be drawn. The earliest cycle is the Mythological Cycle. This contains stories of gods and goddesses, the Children of Lir, the voyage of Bran, the Fomorians, the Fir Bolg, the Tuatha Dé Danann and the Celts. Then there is the Ulster Cycle, which includes Cú Chulainn, Queen Maedhbh and the *Táin*. Thirdly, there is the Finn Cycle, which tells of Fionn McCumhail, Oisín, the Fianna and all their many exploits. Fourthly, there is the Historical Cycle, recounting the time of Tara and the High Kings.

Within this framework one can find visionary journeys, battles between light and darkness, deep psychological insights, spiritual wisdom and magic, as well as beautiful human stories of tragedy and romance, heroism and betrayal. These stories have been handed down to us by people who valued their content and who were nourished by the spiritual food they provided. These stories are there to be told. If telling them around the fire is a practice that has died out, what better place to tell them today than among a gathering for worship?

One particular story, for example, reputedly recounted by Tuán Mac Cearúil to St Finian of Clonard, tells of the five invasions of Ireland prior to Christianity. In this story we have the framework for Ireland's Old Testament: the Partholonians were the first to set foot on the land of Ireland; they had links to Noah – Partholan was Noah's grandson. Next came the Nemedians, about whom we know very little. After them came the Fir Bolg, who got their name from carrying bags full of clay around their middles. Then the Tuatha Dé Dannan, that noble race of people who were half-human, half-divine. And finally the Milesians or Celts, who brought us the druidic traditions and the Brehon Laws.[1]

Stories Concerning the Transition to Christianity
There is a large collection of stories that are situated in the period of transition from pre-Christian to Christian in Ireland.

The story of Tuán above is but one example. Other stories tell of the pre-Patrician saints (Declan, Ciarán, Ailbe and Ibar) and how Christianity was in Ireland before Patrick. And of course there are stories of Patrick himself at the Hill of Tara and elsewhere. These stories are worth recounting as they indicate how the transition from pagan to Christian was understood to have happened. As we recount them today, we too can build into them our understanding of what may have happened.

Stories from the Lives of the Irish Saints

The greatest collection of stories from the Celtic Christian era are about the Irish saints. These saints had a character and an identity that was distinctly Irish. Their understanding of Church, their spirituality, their politics and their culture were all indigenous. Stories of these Irish saints carry within them the distinctive qualities of the Irish character, the history of the people, and an explanation for marks on the Irish landscape that have been left by them.

There are also many rarely recounted stories of Irish monks who travelled to Europe. These stories are often remembered in the places where they settled –– France, Belgium, Germany, Austria, Italy, Switzerland – rather than here in Ireland. They tell of a glorious period in Ireland's history, when the Irish were the saviours of the cultural and spiritual heritage of Europe. Now that Ireland is again involved in Europe in a constructive way, these stories can offer inspiration, wisdom and guidance.

Landscape as a Resource for Worship

The second great resource for worship is the Irish landscape. Ireland has a breathtaking beauty that invites us to worship. If we gather outside in the open air, we come directly in touch with the four elements of life – air, fire (the sun), earth and water. We also come in touch with the four directions. In this setting, it can be easier to see the context of our own lives, situated within nature. It can be easier to acknowledge our dependence on these elements for life itself. As we worship surrounded by nature, we can sense the divine presence in all of creation. We can join with all created beings in worshipping. Whether we worship outside during the day or during the night, we place ourselves in the cathedral created by the hand of God. There can be no finer cathedral anywhere.

Worshipping Outdoors at Times of Transition

In the Celtic tradition, it is believed that the divine is particularly accessible at dawn or dusk, noon or midnight. These are the transition times in the day, just as Halloween night, the Equinox and the Solstices are transition times in the year. At transition times, the division between this world and the Otherworld gets thin and it is possible to intercommunicate or even to travel from one world to the other. When one worships outdoors at these times, one can have a clear sense of these moments of transition. We can then open ourselves to transition in our own lives, and this can bring about grace-filled changes within us.

Our History Written in the Landscape

Our history has been written on the landscape.

When we worship outdoors, we not only see the hand and experience the presence of the Divine in nature, but we also have an opportunity to get directly in touch with our ancestors who lived on this land before us.

Previous generations have marked out for us the sacred hills and wells, the pilgrim paths and holy islands. They have left on the landscape the dolmens, standing stones, ring forts, round towers, stone crosses, churches and monasteries that remind us of our spiritual heritage.

We can connect also with the suffering and tragedies of our ancestors: the famine graves; the *cillíns* or unconsecrated burial places for unbaptised children; the derelict *botháns* or hovels, where often nine and ten children were reared on milk and potatoes; the Mass rocks in remote places; the locations of drownings, burnings, hangings, murders and accidents.

Connecting with our ancestors through their marks on the landscape is an act of worship, as was the recording in the Bible of the story of the Hebrews. Remembering our history and reflecting on it in the light of God's love is a healthy spiritual exercise.

Irish Music, Dance and Language as a Resource for Worship
Thirdly, in the Celtic tradition in Ireland, we have a wealth of cultural heritage that is available to us to enrich our spiritual lives. Irish traditional music, and other forms of Irish music, contain deep expressions of the soul of Ireland and of its people. Other expressions of that soul are to be found in traditional dancing, singing, and in the many traditional arts and crafts.

Perhaps most of all, the soul of the people of Ireland is to be found in the Irish language. Yet words are not enough to give expression to the deepest movements of the heart. Irish monks lay prostrate on the ground, held their hands in the air, walked neck-deep in water, journeyed across land and sea, lived on the top of mountains, fasted for long periods and generally went to any extreme to know God and find their 'place of resurrection'. Our worship can be a place where the search continues, where new ways of opening up to the spirit are tested, where we use dance and music, art and crafts, to channel what cannot be channelled in words.

In order to put some flesh on the ideas above, I describe below how one might put together a Mass based on the Celtic tradition.

Suggestions for a Mass Based on the Celtic Heritage

Leadership

In this celebration, I suggest the leadership is a shared balance between men and women. In this way, the vision of a reconciled gender balance is given a clear expression.

Gathering

Gather outdoors at a natural beauty spot or at a place with some sacred connection. Begin with some music, singing, dancing.

Turas Deiseal / Walk Sunwise

Traditionally, the *turas deiseal* is the most suitable way to begin. This is a circular walk 'to the right'. It makes most sense when it is done around a holy well, standing stone, or old church. It can also be done in an open field, or around a fire, a tree or an altar.

The *turas deiseal* suggests pilgrimage or journey. It is done to the right, imitating the sun as it appears to travel across the sky from east to west in the northern hemisphere. In doing this ritual, you tune-in with the rhythms of the earth, the cycle of days, the seasons and the passing years. The *turas deiseal* traditionally blesses the place being walked upon, as well as the person doing the walking. One does the round seven times, counting with pebbles, which are held in the hand. While doing this, songs may be sung or music played.

Invocation of God's Presence

Traditionally, this is the Sign of the Cross in the name of the Trinity. It can be added to by calling up the presence of Mother Earth, the trinitarian Celtic goddess Anu or Brigit, or other ancient Celtic gods and goddesses.

An example: In the name of the Father, Son and Holy Spirit; in the name of the Mother, the Maiden and the Wise Woman (*Máthair, Maighdean agus Cailleach Feasa*).

This example seeks to balance the male and female energies in the worship and puts a feminine as well as masculine face on God.

Chant/Drumming

Certain activities can draw us into a 'recollected state' or alter our state of consciousness. Drumming and chanting are two such activities. Chanting can be a simple humming or 'ohm' sound, using deep slow breathing, or it can be more like charismatic praise in tongues, or it can be similar to 'keening' as was done at Irish wakes in the past. In order for this to be truly worshipful, people should stay in tune with each other and be sensitive to the overall sound. It can be very powerful and transformative.

Silence

Prayer embedded in silence helps us to assimilate all that is being shared and to savour it before moving on.

Prayer

This prayer is traditionally the 'Collect' – a prayer that gathers from the atmosphere created by all the participants, and from the context of the time and the place. One person addresses the spiritual world on behalf of all. It is better spontaneous, although themes can be worked out in advance.

Story-Telling

People are invited to tell a story. Sources to draw from can include the Bible, the Irish tradition, other wisdom traditions and personal stories. Some stories may need to be prepared in advance. For example, if it would be appropriate to tell a story about Fionn McCumhaill, one might approach a suitable participant beforehand, ask him/her to read the story in advance, and then come and tell it in his/her own words.

A story told is nearly always better than a story read. This applies to the Gospels and other Bible stories also. They are better told than read – and of course this is how they originally were communicated, before they were written down.

Stories can be chosen to connect to a theme, a season, or a point on the spiritual calendar. For example, if the celebration is taking place close to or on an Irish saint's feast day, it might be appropriate to tell a story about that saint.

> Invite people's own stories.
> Invite comment and some discussion.
> Intersperse stories with psalms, poetry, music, dance.

Prayers of Thanksgiving and Intercession

The gathering is invited to contribute prayers of thanksgiving and intercession. A sung response will allow all the prayers to hang together. Soft music can be played by a musician in the background throughout. Those who do not wish to pray publicly can be encouraged to pray privately.

Prayers of intercession are often greatly assisted by some visual action. For example, a stone with a hole in it is a traditional wishing stone in Ireland. Such a stone can be used for intercession. A flower can be passed through it as each intercession is made, or a person can simply hold the stone, pray, and then pass it on. Alternatively, a little altar can be prepared, where people can place objects that represent their prayers.

The Eucharistic Meal

Traditionally, the Eucharistic Meal has been a memorial, a sacrifice, a sharing and a celebration. In a Celtic celebration, it can be all of these things and more. On a particular occasion, one can choose to give emphasis to one aspect over another. Treating this tradition creatively means not allowing oneself to become or remain stuck in rigid patterns. I present here one possibility.

The Eucharistic Meal as we know it had its roots in the Jewish Passover meal. This was a celebration and a remembrance of the Hebrew escape from slavery in Egypt. As such, it represents the story of every nation that has had to shake off oppression. For Irish people, it can represent Ireland's achievement of political freedom, and be a remembrance of our colonisation. For Irish people abroad in the diaspora, it can represent their ancestors' successful escape from the oppression of famine and poverty. For individuals, it can represent elements of their own personal journey, where they have managed to achieve freedom from family oppression, from addiction, from sin. It can also represent the achievement of 'freedom to', rather than just 'freedom from', through learning or new opportunities.

Blessing of the Gifts

An important element of the Eucharistic Prayer is the invitation to the Holy Spirit to 'come upon these gifts'. In an Irish-language version of Eucharistic Prayer II, God is invited to bless the gifts of bread and wine '*le drúcht do Spioraid*' (with the dew of your Spirit). This is a beautiful image from nature, which connects directly into the Celtic belief that dew had magical or sacred properties. Dew was mysterious because no one quite knew how it got on the grass, or how it disappeared from it. Jesus described the Spirit as having these properties (John 3:8).

The dew that is gathered from the grass after dawn is considered Holy in the Celtic tradition. It was traditionally gathered on blankets that were left out overnight, and then wrung out in the morning. If some dew water has been gathered in advance, an imaginative thing to do is to sprinkle it over the bread and put a drop into the chalice.

When praying for the Spirit to come upon the gifts, traditionally the priest or minister places his hands above the gifts. This signifies the understanding that the Spirit comes from above and descends upon the gifts. While this image has a long and authentic history to it, there is, I believe, a need to balance it with the more obvious observation that life-giving transformative power also emerges from the soil, from below. Particularly in springtime, there is an amazing upheaval in the earth that transforms dead-looking seeds and roots into a blaze of growth and colour.

The early Celtic monks were aware of this when they built their monasteries and altars on positive energy points (using dousing methods) or on the tombs of the saints. Many of their chalices had precious gems inserted beneath the base. The gems were not visible to those attending the Eucharist so could not have been for ornamentation. Their function may have been to direct the transforming energy of the earth up into the chalice from below the altar.

In order to express this belief that Mother Earth along with the Holy Spirit provides a life-giving divine energy that is transformative, the hands of a leader could be placed facing upwards beneath the bread and wine, while praying for this transformation to take place.

Sharing the Meal

As an immediate preparation for sharing the sacred meal, the Our Father is said or sung and the Sign of Peace given. A variation on the latter is for the Sign of Peace to be kept to the very end. Doing it this way means it does not have to be cut short for people to go back to their places and it allows the floodgates of chatter and laughter to open and stay open.

Bringing the Ceremony to an End

After the sharing of the meal together, it is a good time to sit in silence and meditate. During this silence, things may well-up in people, which they might like subsequently to share. An invitation to sharing after the silence is all that is needed. These sharings are often the richest pickings of the whole event; something equivalent to the twelve baskets of scraps gathered up by the disciples after the feeding of the five thousand (John 6:13). There is room for music and singing here too.

A prayer by a leader brings the sharing and/or silence to an end.

Final Blessing

Traditionally in Ireland, people are blessed by each other as they say goodbye. 'God bless' is the most basic form. In the Irish language there are many other forms – *Go mbeannaí Dia dhuit; Go n-éirí an bóthar leat; Go ngnóthaí Dia dhuit* (God bless you; May the road rise with you; May God prosper you) – as well as some longer versions now so popular with the tourists, for example:

> May the road rise with you.
> May the wind be always at your back.
> May the sun shine warm upon your face.
> May the rain fall soft upon your field.
> Until we meet again, may God hold you in the palm of his/her hand.

One could make a distinction between prayers of protection and prayers of blessing. Both are needed and there are plenty of examples in the Celtic tradition, such as *St Patrick's Breastplate.*[2]

The leader or leaders proclaim the blessings while extending their hands out towards the participants. The latter receive by doing likewise. Alternatively, the whole gathering can form a circle, holding hands, so that the blessings symbolically passes through the circle. In this case, each person turns their right hand upwards and their left hand downwards and joins hands with their neighbours. The blessing then is given with the left hand and received with the right and travels in a *turas deiseal.*

A Celtic Sign of the Cross

The Celtic monks were creative with the Sign of the Cross when they made it in stone. They put their distinctive mark on the horizontal and vertical shafts by integrating a circle into it. This may have represented the sun, seen as the material source of all life.

We can also be creative with the way we make the Sign of the Cross. In the above example of creative liturgy, there is a balancing of dual energies: masculine and feminine. If we make a two-handed Sign of the Cross, we can express this balance of dualities. In a two-handed Sign of the Cross, the two hands together make the sign to the forehead and the diaphragm, and then each hand, separately and simultaneously, goes to the right and left shoulder before joining together to finish. I call this the Celtic Sign of the Cross.

A Spiral Dance

Finally, I suggest a dance to finish with, called 'The Spiral Dance'. In this dance, the people begin in a circle, holding hands, facing into the middle. The symbolism of this spiral dance becomes clearer when it is done. On the journey into the centre, each person is moving in the spiral with his/her back to everyone else. This symbolises the personal journey inwards that each of us has to make alone. On the return journey outwards, people are facing each other as they pass, and all end up facing outwards when the circle finally reforms. This second part of the dance symbolises the journey out into the world that each of us has to make. In terms of our celebration, it breaks up the exclusivity of the group and sends the participants on their way with responsibility and support.

DIGGING FOR SOUND
IN THE CELTIC TRADITION

Nóirín Ní Ríain

Anthropologists agree that people of all creeds, colours and cultures have a song, a music, which is the very essence of their society and being. Likewise, every world community has its own spiritual expression. Furthermore, the interaction between song and spirituality is vital. One balances the other – if only so fleetingly – to allow us to experience a touch of the divine in our lives. And the radical nub of matters here is that this encounter is not exclusive of anybody, any time or any space. But the pertinent question now is how to access, how to dial up or surface that vital net of laying a finger on our own inner soul. So the notion of each one of us becoming a 'sound archaeologist' is born!

There is a sense of being at the exact centre of the perfect circle, the throbbing heart of things, when we peer into the material remains or song/prayer remains of the past. The amount and wealth of these sacred, sound and prayer archaeological sites is unfathomable because singing and spirituality were so closely intertwined for our Celtic foreparents. Just as praying to God while going about one's daily chore-round was habitual, so too singing was almost the measure of success of the many daily jobs to be done.

When it comes to imagining and recreating the sounds, psalms or sacred songs of our foreparents, something else is triggered off – a new and unexplored discography of the imagination – *soul is unleashed.* It is the archaeology of my own personal discography of psalm and sound that I want to share here.

Sing Me the Creation

Let me preface that personal dig with a song-story artifact thrown up by an early 'sound archaeologist', the Venerable Bede (AD 672-735). In his famous *Ecclesiastical History of the English People*, Bede relates the story of the poet, Caedmon. One evening, after supper, as the harp was being passed about among his singing friends, Caedmon, conscious of his inability to sing, slipped outside. He fell asleep in an outhouse, where an angel appeared to him in a dream, asking him to sing a song.

Refusing again, the angel pressed Caedmon further to sing just for him.

'But what will I sing?' asked the shy poet.
'Sing me the creation,' the angel replied.

And Caedmon, in his sleep that night, composed and sang the first of many hymns that he was to create from then on.[1]

'The Quick of My Life'

Singing has been the quick of my life and existence, my well-being and health – my whole reality. The words 'heal' and 'health' take their source from the Germanic word *Xailaz,* which means 'whole'. It is in this sense that song and its re-creation through performance are inextricably bound in one another for me and totally interconnected.

Sometimes, throughout my life, this interconnectedness has been perfectly in balance, like the seemingly haphazard yet finely tuned and timed appearance of the first snowdrop pushing its head gently yet firmly above the winter snows. Sometimes it has been in constant flux and dialogue, as in the necessary tension between light and shadow, good and evil, male and female, the microcosm and the macrocosm. Yet the driving mission in singing both for myself and for others is best articulated briefly by a proverb from the Irish tradition; a proverb, from the Latin *PRO+verbum*, meaning 'a set of words put out there', or *seanfhocal* (an old word – as we say in Irish) that has a huge amount to say to us today. These proverbs are the miniature, inspired poems of our foremothers and forefathers, whittled down or chiselled away for centuries to bind us together, to teach us the deepest truths, mindless of time, culture, creed and life experience. The proverb I refer to runs as follows:

> *Mo Scéal Féin – Scéal Gach Duine*
> My Own Story – Everybody's Story

Inspired and touched by this deep adage, I offer part of my story here, my own digging for sound and soul, in the hope of the reader resonating with something within it.

Foundation Stones

Praying, like singing, has been for me a constant, woven into childhood, schooling, childrearing days and nights. Characteristic of my youthful spirituality – and perhaps it is innately characteristic of any childish, undeveloped belief – was an almost exclusive preoccupation with just one element of prayer – the attribute of petition and intercession. Adoration, thanksgiving, confession, were all the other prayer facets to come much later.

My memories of youth recall a total confidence in a God who daily answered all my prayers, and I stood tall and upright directly between Him and my world of temporal needs of the moment – be they for a driving test (which I got first time round!), or a three-day pilgrimage to Lough Derg to barter God in exchange for finding me a life-partner and father to my children! Not to mention getting on my knees to say nine Hail Marys to St Anne every Tuesday for a surprise!

Sometimes these two soul-stirring pursuits of singing and praying came together, as I vividly recall quietly crooning 'Tantum Ergo' at the close of the secret Mass which I 'said' every afternoon after school in the careful privacy of my parent's bedroom at the age of seven. Or later on in the evening, when my job was to 'close in' the hens, I would lull them to rest firstly with 'Soul of My Saviour' and then we would say the 'Our Father' together. I believed then, in my own childish reasoning, that those beady, flickering eyes and the high-pitched, nasal hen-sounds were in perfect harmony in our duet of prayer.

Boarding secondary-school days revolved around a balance between singing and praying – at morning Masses, Holy Hours, Benediction and so on – and this often lonely, five-year spell deepened some kind of compensation or ulterior bonding between both song and soul which still haunts me now. University days saw me make my way to the protective, womb-like atmosphere of the Honan Chapel in Cork for midday daily Mass, and again music formed the backdrop. I sometimes played the rickety organ, sometimes sang the psalm, and God forgive me for the many times I innocently and guilelessly urged and taunted my devout student colleagues to 'sing up' in the spirit of the Ambrosian cant – *Bis orat qui cantat* (The one who sings, prays twice!).

Many's the day back then too when at the moment of *Ite Missa Est*, the final Mass blessing, I craned my neck down to the back of that same hallowed space in anticipation of the presence of the young man I was to marry – after the Lough Derg spells!

And indeed through this relationship, music and spirituality have come alive, at so many key moments, too numerous and irrelevant to relate here – keeping us through thick and thin. Enough girlhood nostalgia now! The deepest communion of song and prayer was yet to be born, yet to be discovered and studied, in the decade spanning my thirties and this millennium's 1980s.

Isn't it strange that as you walk through life, you get no map, have no sense of direction for most of it. But then, in later life, you're divinely lifted to the top of the mountain on the clearest, Solstice-sun-filled morning and turned gently around to behold the miraculous landscape of your being. The trials and tribulations fade into the mists of time and slip softly from the memory. As I scan that panorama of my life, I realise I was being prepared for this tunnel of song in a very unconscious and subtle, God-given manner, which now makes perfect serendipitous sense.

Magical Influence of Ancient Song Form

My *sean-nós*[2] guru during the decade previous to the eighties was a Corkman, Pilib Ó Laoghaire, who was steeped in the luscious, mellifluous *Déise* tradition of County Waterford.[3] Through this wild rose of song folklore, he mesmerised me, when I often literally sat at his feet while he, note by note, beautiful word by word, passed me on his repertoire, his *stór amhrán*. A song that melted into my soul, from the moment he first sang it or, as we say, 'turned' it for me one May Saturday morning, was the haunting '*Seacht nDólás na Maighdine Muire*' (The Seven Sorrows of Mary). I could not let go of its magic ever again and I share it visually with you now. Even the very architecture of the written note thrills the eye like a work of art: the basic five-line stave, which always seems to mirror ley lines or the Aboriginal song lines, guiding and guarding the course of the sound; the notes like little circular beings with arm outstretched, sometimes up to the heavens, sometimes down into the earth. The story of all our lives!

(See footnote 4)

Three Rivers of Song and Prayer-Story

This one song was to become the pool source of three meandering rivers of song and prayer-story. The first river takes its source from a little pool of a very rich, intimate repertoire of traditional religious songs in Irish. It began in 1979 when I embarked upon a postgraduate degree in this area of research. For me, this was such a special time; I was that 'sound archaeologist' involved in a most precious dig, which would transform my whole life from then on.

Caoineadh na Maighdine (The Virgin's Lament)

At precisely that time, a very important music friendship of prayer and song flowered for me with the Benedictine community of Glenstal Abbey in my home county of Limerick, a friendship that is still alive and well today twenty years on. This pool of spirituality and song overflowed and took on a course of its own in the form of the first of three joint recordings. *Caoineadh na Maighdine* embodies eleven precious gems from this Irish tradition, resounded in the sonorous, reverberating acoustic of the Glenstal Church. From my heart, I wrote at that time:

> The actual performance of these songs in Glenstal Abbey has meant more to me than just making the kind of record which normally marks one's musical progress and area of interest at a particular time. Stereotyped studios, seas of microphones, time pressures and endless 'takes', had no part in this setting of religious music.
>
> The absence of such features, which inevitably accompany the average recording, opened up the possibility of making this performance the most personalised and sincere outcry of the singer, for whom each phrase of a song is a constant confession or expression of being.
>
> For the twelve monks who accompany me on this record, singing is a powerful medium of prayer inextricably bound up with their daily lives. Such a background has had an indelible influence on my own singing. None of these songs will ever exist for me as an isolated piece of music.
>
> Woman speaks strongly through the religious songs of Ireland. She comes alive and breathes forth an antithesis: sometimes overpoweringly Christian, sometimes lulling

the child of God to sleep within her life, sometimes bitterly questioning the right of this same God to claim her child. Such emotions have immeasurably transformed not only my approach to singing, but also something within me which goes far deeper and defies articulation.[5]

Good People All

The second tributary of sound, two years later, takes its name, *Good People All*, from the timeless, enigmatic tradition of Christmas carols still sung in south-east Wexford in the parish of Kilmore. Following an almost unbroken three-hundred-year-old tradition of song and singing, we sang our hearts out to God again through another eleven hymns of praise. This is a recording of light and darkness, day and night, because sometimes in the chapel we whispered our praises in song into just one microphone, in between the daily monastic round of the monastery. Sometimes we sang late into the night in that same space in almost complete darkness, with candlelight dancing around us, bringing the best out in us!

Vox De Nube (A Voice from the Cloud)

The third river recording enveloped these two preceding tributaries of sound and ran boldly into the worldwide sea, as we made our final trilogical statement. *Vox de Nube* was our tribute to world spiritual music and we looked and sang outwards through a collection of Plain Chant, visionary music of a contemporary Swiss woman Joa Bolendas, Byzantine chant, and the inspired hymns of twelfth-century German Benedictine Abbess, Hildegard Von Bingen. For this disc of praise, I made the pilgrimage back to my prayer-space of college days, the Honan Chapel, to crystallise and call down the twenty universal sacred songs at the Michaelmas feast of 1989.

Time stood still for those few hours. Not only did we feel that Michael the Archangel was blessing us, but the angel of the Annunciation and Raphael, who are also remembered on this autumn day of 29 September, seemed to join in the sing-song too! One angel trilogy guarded us as we completed another! Our earthly musical guardian angel this day and on the previous other recording days was Mícheál Ó Súilleabháin, and making sense of it all then he wrote:

> Our vision of Western chant has come about through a subversion of a thousand-year-old manuscript tradition. The voice, 'like a thing's heart' searches the depths of aural consciousness for something of the music's original breath. Masked – perhaps even protected – by an eclectic repertoire, flashes of emotive colour surge through the sound surprising us like wild flowers among the rocks. As the branch greens, as the cactus flowers, we are challenged to break ground from beneath.
>
> The incisive voice is the perfect means of cutting a way through the overgrowth, and the Word reverberates to this voice of praise inviting us to link Earth with Heaven. Under the light of the Voice from the Cloud we are drawn into God's own time.[6]

Revelation About Him – *Vox De Nube, Vox Populi, Vox Clamantis in Deserto* – From the Cloud, People and Earth

That same aural experience which true chant and true prayer share on some deep level and which fused and wedded this trilogy tale of the eighties is closed in a nutshell in all three song testimonies by philosopher, Benedictine monk and singer Mark Patrick Hederman, and I leave the last word on this trilogy of sacred songs to him.

In our Judaeo-Christian tradition God has always remained in a cloud of unknowing. Revelation about Him has been aural: a voice from the cloud (*Vox de Nube*) or a voice crying in the wilderness.

The voices that speak for or about him are either from this cloud, from this earth or from his people. In this recording there are echoes of all three, but the emphasis here is on the voice from that cloud of unknowing, expressed in the Latin Plainchant or revealed by two mystics, one from the twelfth century and one from our own times, Hildegard of Bingen and Joa Bolendas. This recording is the third in a trilogy of such voices: *Vox de Nube, Vox Populi* (Good People All) and *Vox Clamantis in Deserto* (Caoineadh na Maighdine).[7]

A Gust Inside the God

In my musical and spiritual journey, marked by these blessed islands of sound – these three CD recordings from Glenstal Abbey – I was digging for my own sound, often without realising it myself. What was my guiding star in that sacred digging? What held me on that star path? What voice guided me from the cloud of my unknowing self?

I leave the last word to the Prague-born poet Rainer Maria Rilke, who spins and weaves the many multi-coloured threads onto a tapestry of feeling through this *Sonnet to Orpheus*.

A God can do it. But will you tell me how
a man can penetrate through the lyre's strings?
Our mind is split. And at the shadowed crossing
of heart-roads, there is no temple for Apollo.

Song, as you have taught it, is not desire,
not wooing any grace that can be achieved;

song is reality. Simple for a god.
But when can we be real? When does he pour

the earth, the stars, into us? Young man,
it is not your loving, even if your mouth
was forced wide open by your voice – learn

to forget that passionate music. It will end.
True singing is a different breath, about
nothing. A gust inside the God. A wind.[8]

THE BLACKBIRD AND THE BELL
REFLECTIONS ON THE CELTIC TRADITION

John Moriarty

The following is a transcript of a conversation between myself (Padraigín Clancy) and John Moriarty on Celtic spirituality, conducted at his home in County Kerry. As a philosopher and story-teller, John's primary medium is the oral/bardic tradition. I decided to record *the word* as spoken by him. My questions and comments are written in bold.

Where are we situated exactly, John?
Under Mangerton Mountain, down from the Horses' Glen, with Torc in front of us and Dá Chích Anann [the Paps of Anu] out here to the east of us, and west of us here we have Teamhair Luachra, which is Cú Roí Mac Dáire's place – the highest cashel in Ireland.[1]

And the darkness is closing in around us!
Yes – coming up to mid-summer 1999.

We were talking earlier about the word 'Celtic' – what are your own reflections on what is happening in Ireland on the threshold of the third millennium – the kind of searching that is taking place and the emergence of the Celtic once again?
Well, I have a feeling that the crisis that is now facing humanity at large and facing the whole earth and everything that lives on it, so great is the crisis, I think we now have to meet it creatively – falling back on the old traditions is not enough. The crisis is different and of a bigger order than I think humanity has ever

previously had to cope with. While there is wisdom in the various traditions, including the Celtic, and we daren't go forward into the future without it, we must now be *originally* creative.

I mean the earth has voyaged for 4,600 million years; that is a long voyage. It has voyaged with the Tribulite; it has voyaged with Tyrannosaurus, it has voyaged with Dinosaurus, and now the earth is voyaging with humanity.

It seems to me that the earth has now crashed into an iceberg and we, the human species, are the iceberg into which it has crashed, and it might be that the earth will not survive the crash – that is how serious I believe the situation is.

This to me calls for a totally creative response. We now as a people have to get to the place where myths are born and we have to allow new myths and a new vision to emerge. And we won't do that by inventing a past for ourselves.

Do you think we are inventing a past for ourselves in going back to the Celtic tradition?

Yes, I think that is what some people are doing with the Celtic tradition. First they are inventing the past, then they are going back into it – that is not going to shelter us or help us.

How is the past being invented?

Well, for example, right now it is fashionable to see wonders in the Celtic stuff – in the Celtic tradition. And there are wonders in it, but it also has its quorum of darkness which should be recognised.

I mean I grew up in North Kerry. I remember a day when my father came into the house fairly white-faced because he had been back the west field and he had opened a wind of hay and found four bad eggs inside in it.[2] He then took his four-pronged fork and put a raft of hay on top of the four prongs, and he was praying as he did so.[3] He walked to the river with the four eggs and he put the raft on the river. He slid the fork out from under the raft and he allowed the river to carry the evil off his land.

Now the four bad eggs in the middle of the hay – they were put there by someone who had malintentions; that was the practice of the *piseoga* [casting spells]. It was sympathetic magic; the four bad eggs in the land will create its image and likeness. It will turn that which is alive into badness. I mean the old principle is that like creates like. Bad meat or eggs on the land will create bad land.

Nowadays people look to the Celtic Christian tradition and we find when we look at it that there are many prayers for protection in it – *orthaí cosanta*. In *St Patrick's Breastplate*, Patrick surrounds himself; above, below, to his right and to his left; he covers himself totally in a shield of protection:

> *Críst lim, Críst reum, Críst im degaid,*
> *Críst indium, Críst íssum, Críst úasum,*
> *Críst dessum, Críst túathum....*[4]

> Christ with me, Christ before me, Christ behind me,
> Christ in me, Christ below me, Christ above me,
> Christ on my right, Christ on my left....

Why? Why has Patrick so fastidiously covered himself? It must be because he felt threatened, and I believe he did feel threatened.[5]

If you remember the story of *Balar of the Evil Eye;* where did he get that evil eye from?[6] How did it happen? It happened one day when he was walking past a window and the fumes of a fantastic cauldron that the druids were brewing, came up and hit his eye, and poisoned the eye. Now he had the *súil mhillteach* [evil eye] ever after.

So there was evidently some fantastic stuff being brewed in that cauldron – fiercely effective. I mean it was like the Australian Aborigines pointing a bow – it had the power to kill, the power to destroy, to do huge damage. It is possible that there are energies, nature spirits, or whatever it is, that you can get on the wrong side of, and they are actually helping you to do terrible things.

So people talk about the Book of Kells as if it existed on its own, but there were books of spells and charms as well, and Patrick and his contemporaries knew this.

We admire the Ardagh Chalice and it is wondrous in its sacramental loveliness, but the shadow side of the Ardagh Chalice is the witches' cauldron we read about in Shakespeare's *Macbeth*. I mean Macbeth is a Celt and it is a Celtic play set in Scotland. Macbeth comes upon the witches' cauldron and he is unable to cope with what is going on there – he cannot handle the witches and those dark energies. I mean here are their words:

> Fillet of a fenny snake,
> In the cauldron boil and bake;
> Eye of newt and toe of frog,
> Wool of bat and tongue of dog,
> Adder's fork and blind worm's sting,
> Lizard's leg and howlet's wing,
> For a charm of powerful trouble,
> like a hell-broth boil and bubble.
>
> Double, double, toil and trouble;
> Fire burn and cauldron bubble.[7]

So I would want to say there is at least as much darkness in the Celtic tradition as there is light – and that the Celts were aware of moral duality. The Irish tale *Battle of Magh Tuiredh* is the old Indo-European battle; the battle between good and evil. This same battle was fought in India, Greece, Scandinavia and Ireland. In India it was between the gods [Devas] and anti-gods [Assuras]. In Greece it was fought between a younger generation of gods or giants and an older generation. In Scandinavia it was fought between the Aesir and Vanir. In Ireland it was fought between the Fomhoire [demons] led by Balar and the Túatha Dé Danann [divine people] led by Lugh.

So when people look back and see loveliness everywhere, their eyes are simply not open, they are creating a fiction.

Darkness, therefore, is an intrinsic part of the Celtic tradition, as it is of the whole human story?

Yes – it is sentimental to believe there are not or were not dark energies around. There will always be darkness as well as light. There will always be the struggle of light against darkness because we human beings are the kind of creatures we are.

I mean we have lived in a very dark century – a century when you stand in Auschwitz is really a century when you have to take evil into account. To stand in Auschwitz is to have your backbone turned into a question mark about the nature of the human being.

The people of the enlightenment of the French revolution and Russian revolution thought that evil was a consequence of bad social organisation. Now Dostoevsky argued against this. He said that evil is radical in the school; by radical he means 'of the root'.

So in our struggle with evil we need divine assistance. We need something as old-fashioned as sanctifying grace – we need sacramental help. Patrick knew this so he had to put on the Breastplate as he journeyed into 'the heart of darkness'. He had to become sacramentally invulnerable to the powers he was dealing with. At least this was the perception of his early monastic biographers. This is the kind of energy Muirchú saw him as having to deal with.[8]

So, you believe we need divine assistance?

Yes, talking about Christian assistance or divine assistance as Christians understand it, I sometimes refer to how the ice cap comes down over the Arctic ocean and into the Arctic lands at the beginning of autumn, and how seals have to keep breathing-holes open in the ice because they are mammals. They have to come up to breathe. They have to go down for food and then they have to come up and haul themselves on to the ice in order to breathe.

I would see the sacraments of the Christian religion for instance as being like the seals' breathing-holes. Human beings need to breathe grace. We just don't need to breathe oxygen, we need to breathe sanctifying grace. We need to take grace into ourselves. What I am saying is as old-fashioned as the old Christian doctrine of nature and grace – not grace eliminating nature but grace transforming nature – and that for me is the Christian way of talking about what we have to do.

If you were to ask me about religion in Ireland I would begin to locate the heart of it in the poem *Lon Dubh An Chairn* [The Blackbird of Derry Carn]. There you have Oisín, the old pagan, saying that nature – symbolised by the call of the Irish totemic bird, the blackbird – is where we've got to find healing and magnificence and significance; where we find our true worth. Then you have Patrick ringing the bell, which calls us to transcendence. So you have the wrestling between immanence and transcendence. Now it seems to me that there is something wonderful, a kind of healing, in listening to the blackbird, but in the end it isn't a final healing, in the end we have to listen to the bell.[9]

Do you think the exultation of the early monks in relation to nature excludes the darkness?

Yes, many early Irish lyrics show that the Celtic monks were listening to the lovely voice of the blackbird, and it has a beautiful voice – the thrush is full of hysteria in comparison. Take the ninth-century anonymous poem, 'The Black Bird by Belfast Loch' [*Lon Dubh ós Loch Laíg*]:

> *Int én bec*
> *ro leic feit*
> *do rinn guip*
> *glanbuidi:*
> *Fo-ceird faíd*
> *ós loch laíg,*
> *lon do chraíb*
> *charnbuidi*

> The little bird which has whistled
> From the end of a bright
> – yellow bill; it utters a note
> above Belfast Loch – a blackbird
> From a yellow-heaped branch[10]

This is a lovely poem in monosyllables, with each of the two stanzas ending polysyllabically. It is a perfect example of a poem of monosyllabic and polysyllabic wonder and splendour about the lovely note of the blackbird – in its way it is as perfect as the Ardagh Chalice, a delight, a wonderful poem! But we look at that lovely bird an hour later and that yellow bill from which the lovely note comes has three or four worms in its mouth. That bill is now like a butcher shop and the blackbird is taking those worms back to his brood, do you know what I mean? Then, we realise that according to

Darwin's theory of evolution that – hang on – this blackbird is a feather dinosaur.

The Celtic monks did not see the blackbird from the point of view of the worms in its lovely bill, or if they did they didn't write about it, and it is because we do not see the blackbird as the feather dinosaur that we need to hear the bell.

More recently, writers in the English language such as Emily Brontë and William Wordsworth have been accused of similar romanticism. Emily Brontë in a kind of Romantic manifesto talks about walking out into nature and finding final healing:

> I'll walk, but not in old heroic traces
> And not in paths of high morality,
> And not among the half-distinguished faces,
> The clouded forms of long-past history.
>
> I'll walk where my own nature would be leading–
> It vexes me to choose another guide–
> where the grey flocks in ferny glens are feeding,
> where the wild wind blows on the mountain side.
>
> What have these lonely mountains worth revealing?
> More glory and more grief than I can tell:
> The earth that wakes one human heart to feeling
> Can centre both the worlds of heaven and hell.[11]

Wordsworth in the 'Lucy Poems' talks about nature taking over almost from the biblical God, and re-creating Lucy, this girl who lives in the dales – nature shall re-make her as a beautiful creature:

> …the floating clouds their state shall lend
> To her; for her the willow bend;

Nor shall she fail to see
Even in the motions of the storm
Grace that shall mould the Maiden's form
By silent sympathy[12]

Now it has been said that Wordsworth lived in a beautiful part of the world – in the northern temperate zone, where nature is largely domesticated. If Wordsworth had lived in the tropics he couldn't possibly have written that kind of poem, because there, nature is much more terrifying, much more savage. And it isn't terrifying because there are pumas or jaguars – it is because of all the insects. If I were to crash on a plane tomorrow morning into the Amazon, it is likely that it wouldn't be the jaguars would get me, it is probable it would be the insects.

It is as if some of the people talking presently about the Celtic thing have never actually looked at the mouth of a crocodile – the sheer fantastic loneliness of the mouth of a crocodile – and that is nature!

So, I would like to say there are a lot of lies going around about the Celtic thing. The first lie is that it is all lovely. Each sentence we use in relation to the Celtic has to be prefaced by the word 'lovely'. The second lie is that there is no dualism in the Celtic world, and the third lie is that the Celts believed there was total and final healing in nature – if they did, it was because they had not seen the terror of nature, it was because they couldn't see the blackbird as the feather dinosaur.

I see, in humanity and in the Celtic tradition, a constant struggle between a dual allegiance; an allegiance to the blackbird and an allegiance to the bell. The blackbird summoning us to immanence and the bell summoning us to transcendence, and I would want to say myself that I believe we must listen to the bell.

What Do You Find Inspirational About The Celtic Tradition?

What's great you know about the whole Celtic thing is that if you take the simple idea, for instance that all the rivers of Ireland have their source in an Otherworld well – whether it is Conaire's well or the well of Nechtan or whoever – they all rise in an Otherworld: that to me is wonderful.[13]

I mean geographers, ordinary, modern, secular geographers would tell you precisely where the Shannon rises, where the Liffey rises, where the Blackwater rises. But in another sense they rise in eternity, the whole universe rises in eternity. We all have our sources in an Otherworld well; every blade of grass has its source in eternity, not in ordinary time at all!

There was one day back in the Dingle peninsula. It was a very calm evening. There was mist on the mountains and the sea was a yogi; it had gone out in a total bliss of contemplation. There was mist on Mount Brandon, it was as soft as rabbit fur on top and there was blue under it. The only sound on the Dingle peninsula that evening was the sound of a stream coming down Sliabh an Iolair [Eagle Mountain]. And down on the road was Peig Sayers' son Mike File [the poet] – and with him was a *stráinséir* [stranger] – *a lá breá*[14] – and the *stráinséir* drew attention to the silence and the sound; the sound of the stream coming down Sliabh an Iolair. Mike File listened to it for a while and then he said:

> *Tá sé ag glaoch orainn isteach sa síoraíocht as a bhfuil sé féin ag teacht.*
> It is calling us into the eternity, out of which it is coming.

Now that sense is wonderful to me, and in so far as the Celtic tradition knows that all the rivers of Ireland have their source in an Otherworld well and that a hazel tree overgrows that well, and that kernels of wisdom are going to fall from that hazel down into the well, and that they are eaten and carried downstream by the salmon who swims out of this ordinary world into the Otherworld. And that any one of us who eats that *Bradán Feasa* [salmon of knowledge] will become wise, anyone who partakes of this Otherworld wisdom will become wise; that is a wonderful picture of reality. If we could make that live among us, that awareness, then we could walk the earth. Then it would not be possible for us to release the sluice gates of our slurry pits and let the water into our rivers.

The inspiration is in the Irish language too, isn't it?

Yes, when I read Peig Sayers, that language is radiant with a liturgical sense of life. People know in that language how to cross thresholds, how to come into a house and how to go out of a house with reverence and respect. The ordinary language describing ordinary realities in Peig's life is in some way a sacrament of the divine.

The language in Peig Sayers is, for me, as liturgical as the Latin Mass. If I ever wanted to go to Sceilig Mhichíl, that great rock in the ocean where people lived having dedicated themselves to the angel of high places, St Michael, I would first read Peig Sayers, because I feel the liturgical language those monks would have used continues to this century with Peig Sayers.

What masculine archetypes appeal to you in the Celtic tradition?

If you take Yeats. I mean he put Cú Chulainn at the heart of the Celtic revival. I think that was a great pity because Cú Chulainn is not a hero for our day at all. He was a warrior mostly. He suffers from wasting sickness. Women come from the Otherworld and whip him and he endures this wasting sickness for a whole year yet learns nothing from it. And his wife Emer, when she finds out he is sick, talks about going into the dark woods to find a remedy for him. She is willing to go into the dark woods to find a remedy for him. Now Cú Chulainn has no capacity to go into the dark woods – the dark parts of his own psyche or the human psyche – and I often wonder why in God's name anyone was interested in him at all.

I would much prefer to put someone like Fionntan Mac Bóchra or Conaire Caomh or Cú Roí Mac Dáire, anyone that is in touch with and expresses the strange genius of the universe and of the human psyche better than Cú Chulainn ever did. I think that Yeats did us a disservice rather than a service by relocating Cú Chulainn at the heart of the Celtic tradition.

Tell me about Fionntan Mac Bóchra[17]

Well, Fionntan Mac Bóchra. The modern Irish Fionn or Finn is related to the latin *vindos*. It means wisdom. *Mac Bóchra* means Son of the Sea. So already we are dealing with something that is not sociologically describeable. He is the Son of the Sea. He is one of the first men to come ashore in Ireland. When the floodgates open [the biblical deluge] he survives. He transforms himself into a salmon, then into an eagle, then into a hawk. He overflies the whole of Ireland. He knows everything that goes on in Ireland. He is literally the memory of the race.

I think if Yeats had taken him and put him on stage it would have been something significant. However, maybe you couldn't stage him. Maybe he isn't dramatic enough. Cú Chulainn is full of the stupid old drama we are sick of – the cowboy stuff!

One of the discernable elements in the return to the Celtic tradition at the moment is the embracing of the goddess and the archetypes of the feminine. This is very popular, especially among women. Have you any comment to make on that?

Well, the first thing I would want to say is that I have a feeling that we can make too much of the distinctions between male and female. When I am listening to music, for example, to the second movement of Mozart's concerto for piano, harp and flute, it seems to me that I am neither male nor female; I have gone below my hormones, below testosterone, below adrenaline; I've gone below all that characterises me as either male or female. I mean what is male in me and what is female in you is not the whole of what we are. There is a deep in me, there is a deep in you, that is beyond the male and female. This deep is divine ground. That is the first thing I would want to say.

Having said that, I do believe that a ritual distance kept between men and women can help us to understand and appreciate each other better. D. H . Lawrence in *The Woman Who Rode Away*, talks about letting women experience their feminine lunar mysteries and letting men experience their masculine solar mysteries, separately – and I think I agree with that. We can meet but not get mixed up. We are going in for a lot of mixing which is not helpful nowadays. I mean, I think the more a man is a man and the more a woman is a woman the better the chance we have of meeting each other creatively. So ritual distance, I believe, is important.

I am saddened, for example, by the manner in which many women have gone into the workplace. They show themselves to be no wiser than men. In many cases they are imitating men and men's errors and that saddens me greatly. I see women, for example, doing terrible things to their children, just like men, sometimes worse. Pushing them through the modern education system, for example. So I think men and women are equally unwise. I don't join with the current fashion which tends to say everything good is feminine or female and everything terrible is masculine or male. Christianity would say we are both equally fallen and that men and women are equally in need of sanctifying grace.

So, then, to return to the goddess, I would say that healing will come when we return to the deep, to the place where wisdom comes from; a place where music can take us. The deep below what you are as a woman and what I am as a man. That deep is divine ground and from that place we can become truly wise.

What feminine archetypes appeal to you?

The fact that Ireland is named after a goddess is, I believe, a wonderful thing. The fact that in the Celtic tradition the king had to marry the goddess at the *Feis Temro* [Feast of Tara] is very important. A goddess of sovereignty is very important. In a democratic age we are not supposed to talk about sovereignty but I think there are sovereign values and sovereign ways of living. There is something in each of us that is sovereign, that is worldly royal, which never compromises with whatever is cheap and shoddy in the world. If we could only conform to that part of ourselves, then we'd live. First we have to discover our own sovereignty and then walk with it. We meet people who are sovereign in themselves and it is a wonderful place to be.

So that is what the goddess Éire [Ireland] signifies for me; that the Irish people shall be sovereign and shall belong in a sovereign place and live sovereign lives. She upholds the sovereign values so that we, the people, must never be cheapened and never compromise our values. If we are ever cheapened, then we are finished. If the sovereign is killed in us, we die.

I would love to see the day where the Taoiseach would have to formally marry the wise or sovereign part of himself or herself as part of his or her inauguration – just as at the ancient *Feis Temro.*

What are your thoughts on Macha's Curse?

Well, we think nowadays we can go back into the Celtic world or any ancient world and can take that kind of consciousness to ourselves as we take a tin of peas off a supermarket shelf. We cannot do that. So, I imagine the only way back or the only good way back, the only creative way back into the Celtic world or the Celtic consciousness would be if we go back, in and through a rite of passage, *un rite de passage.*

The rite of passage we would go back through as a people would be through the labour pains of the Celtic horse-goddess, Macha. We would be willing to go back and to experience her pain. Then, having suffered with the goddess, we would be worthy and able for the Celtic consciousness and we wouldn't fictionalise or misuse it. Macha's Curse would no longer be experienced or perceived as a curse but would be seen as and experienced as a blessing through which our consciousness could be transformed.

I have often wondered how it was that Christianity caught on so easily in Ireland. I mean there are several reasons: firstly, what the Irish always wanted to hear was a wonder-tale. We, the Celts, were junkies for a wonder-story. Then along comes St Patrick and he talks about a God who opens the sea which whole peoples walk through. And they hear about this God turning water into wine and they are astounded. This God St Patrick talks about is a real *Rí na bhFeart,* a Great God, a king of the stars and wonders of the universe. These were even greater wonders than they were accustomed to hearing about, so they were delighted with the new wonder-tales.

The notion of suffering wasn't such a fantastical idea to them either. Having suffered with the goddess, they were asked at St Patrick's invitation to move over to the idea of suffering – this time with the God called Christ. It wasn't new to them.

How do you see Ireland at present?

In 1839 Daniel O'Connell went to Clifden in Connemara at the Atlantic coast and he talked to a huge gathering of people. He spoke in English and there wasn't even ten people who understood him because Gaeilge or Irish was their language. Exactly a century later, Éamonn De Valera came to Clifden and he spoke in Irish to a huge gathering and there wasn't even ten people who understood him, because English was their language. In that century [nineteenth century] we walked away from the language – in this century [twentieth century] we are walking away, or we think we are walking away, from our religion.

Now, it seems to me in terms of the folk mind, which has an altogether different and older rhythm than the rhythm of linear history, things do not change over a thousand years in the folk mind, it is virtually changeless – it seems to me that to walk away from the language in one century and then to walk away from religion in the next is to walk from an awful lot. What is going to fill the vacuum?

What is filling the (spiritual) vacuum in Ireland?

Consumerism. The virtual reality of the technological world – the Celtic Tiger. Perhaps Balar's evil eye is our poisoned collective eye, *our economic eye*, the poisoned collective eye of humanity.

When the Shah of Iran decided he was going to bring his people into the twentieth century, into the technologies and ideologies of the twentieth century, they said 'no thank you very much' and went back to the seventh century. Now, I am not saying that that is a good thing, but it is what they did.

So! I think having walked away from the language, and from the religion, we could be in for a time of real psychic destabilisation. I think that the place left behind by the language and the religion, could be filled, as such places usually are, by unhelpful energies.

The pursuit of the Celtic is endeavouring to fill the gap?

If we invent a past for ourselves and go back into it, we are not doing ourselves any favours, it is a kind of atavistic impulse. If we go back into the Celtic tradition and open our eyes and see it in its totality, then we can draw on it to help us go forward and, in some respects, as I said earlier, we daren't go forward without it.

But I would still stress: the crisis we are facing now on the earth is so great – so great is the crisis – that we must be *originally* creative. We have to get to the place where myths are born and allow a new vision to emerge.

GLENDALOUGH: A VALLEY OF DREAMS

Michael Rodgers

I am often asked the question, 'Why did you come to Glendalough?' This is usually asked with the expectation that I am going to talk about an inspired vision and plan, with all its parts clearly formed in my mind before I arrived. The truth is that I came to Glendalough because of a longing which could no longer be ignored. It was not so much about doing things or going places any more, but a deep desire to come home and enter into a quieter, contented and more connected place within myself. My inspiration came as much from a mid-life crisis as anything else.

Travelling the empty road over the Wicklow Mountains in September 1992 to find a place to live in Glendalough, I felt alone, vulnerable and full of questions. I had no idea what lay ahead, but in spite of my anxiety I had a sense of freedom that I had not known for a very long time. My thoughts went back to September 1965, when I made my first big break away from home and country. It was harvest time as I said goodbye to the place and people in County Clare that meant so much to me in that first quarter of my life. I set out with their blessing, and the support of St Patrick's Missionary Society, of which I am a member.

Looking back, I can accept with gratitude all the opportunities offered me over the years. Twenty years in Kenya opened up a new vision of things and the enriching experience of living in another culture. As a result of being received and accepted in this different world, I began to realise that I too came from a culture that I had barely acknowledged.

Returning Home: Recognising my Spiritual Heritage

On returning to live in Ireland in 1985, I saw my homeland with new eyes and became fascinated with its ancient history. I visited many of the pre-Christian stone tombs and circles, recognising for the first time something I had always taken for granted, that my ancestors were an important part of who I am. My interest then focused on the Christian heritage of Ireland, from the beehive huts that formed the monastic settlement on faraway Skellig Michael to the beautifully decorated high crosses and round towers scattered all over the Irish countryside. Every visit to those holy places became an experience of pilgrimage. It was a spiritual re-awakening that eventually drew me to live in Glendalough.

In the Footsteps of Kevin

A young man named Kevin entered this enchanted valley of two lakes in the sixth century and decided to build his hermitage here. He recognised the sacred nature of the place and probably found something his soul was seeking deep within it. Out of his experience of solitude, but long after his death, came the inspiration to build a great monastery at a point in the valley where the rivers and roads come together. At that stage Glendalough was established as a place of pilgrimage.

The Celtic people chose places of great natural energy and beauty for their sacred sites and settlements. The three valleys of Glendalough make up one such special place. Two of these lead to open roads eastwards and westwards, while the third is enclosed and surrounded on all sides by steep-sided hills. The whole environment breathes a strong but peaceful presence and the veil between this world and the Otherworld seems almost transparent. The outer landscape connects powerfully with the inner landscape of the pilgrim soul. The journey into the inner valley has special significance in this regard. The first section is in shadow, which is particularly pronounced in winter, when the sun never rises above the high hills of Derrybawn to the south.

Celtic people were sensitive to shadows and darkness, which represented for them danger, fear, evil and the unknown. Their calendar year began at *Samhain* (1 November), as the light faded into midwinter darkness and their twenty-four-hour day began at nightfall, emphasising the importance of the dark hours before the emergence of a new dawn.

Kevin would have been well aware of the forces of darkness when he first set foot in Glendalough. There are many stories told about him which reveal the nature of his journey.

Kevin and the Monster

One story tells of what happened when he came to the first lake, which was then called Loch na Péist (the Lake of the Monster), and came face to face with the monster. He did not ignore or attempt to destroy it but took it with him to the second lake, where he intended to establish his hermitage. This is a very important story.

It has been said that the history of monsters is the story of humanity's struggle to see its own inner face. Kevin made the dramatic choice as a young man to live in solitude. He could not have done this unless he was well acquainted with his weaknesses and strengths, in other words, unless he had confronted and befriended his own inner demons. His decision to take the monster with him came at a moment of enlightenment, which transformed the lake into a place of healing, and gave him the freedom to enter his place of solitude on the shores of the inner lake at a place known in Irish as Díseart Chaoimhín (Kevin's Desert).

Kevin's Rejection of a Beautiful Young Woman

Kevin spent seven years in this desert place. There are many stories of his blessings and disappointments, with angels and devils comforting and tormenting him in turn. The best-known is that of his rejection of the advances of a beautiful young woman. One popular version concludes with the girl being thrown into the lake, where she drowns. It is a sad story and one that distorts the full truth of all we have been told of Kevin's life. Maybe the exaggeration was necessary to demonstrate the difficulty of choosing to renounce the pleasures of human sexuality for God's sake. Such a choice will always result in a painful human struggle.

Kevin and the Blackbird

One of the most attractive stories about Kevin is the one that tells of him praying with outstretched hands for so long that a blackbird came to make a nest and lay an egg in one of them. What was Kevin trying to achieve in those long hours of prayer? Was he seeking unity and balance between the inner life of the heart and the world outside and beyond at the same time? The poet Seamus Heaney refers to Kevin being 'linked into the network of eternal life' at that moment.[1]

Kevin's Desire for Solitude

The desire for solitude is often experienced as an insistent call in the quiet of the heart. Most of us know that feeling at some time or other in our lives. Responding to this call can help us feel more at home in ourselves as well as in the world around us. At the heart of it all is a longing for wholeness, understanding and connectedness.

It is likely that Kevin experienced the blessing of solitude during the seven years he spent in the desert. Fourteen hundred years after his death, his questing spirit lives on in the heart of the Wicklow hills and guarantees its future as a sacred place. Before he died, an angel promised that thousands of monks would follow in his footsteps. That prophecy was fulfilled when Glendalough became a famous monastery, known all over Europe from the sixth to the twelfth centuries. Today there are few monks among the half million people who visit every year but there are still people who seek healing, meaning in life and inner peace.

A Seven-Year Cycle

By September 1999 I will have completed seven years as a resident of Glendalough. According to tradition, this will complete the full cycle of the experience. The longer I am here, though, the deeper the experience becomes and the more there is to discover. I came like a pilgrim with empty hands looking for shelter. The parish priest at that time generously offered me the welcome and hospitality of his house for the first few months. From there I walked every road and pathway and climbed every mountain in the neighbourhood. On a cold February day in 1993 I finally found the ancient site of Kevin's monastery (Teampall na Sceilig) on the shore of the upper lake. I knew then I had come to the real heart of Glendalough and that it would be difficult ever to leave it.

In that same spring, the old *An Óige* youth-hostel was being converted by the new owners into five self-contained apartments. In a step I now see as providential, I rented the first one when it became available. It was an unforgettable moment when I found myself living on the side of Brockagh hill overlooking my valley of dreams and in full view of the high hills of Camaderry, Lugduff and Derrybawn. Below me I could see the Glendasan river winding its way peacefully along the valley floor. People began to hear of my experience and came with requests that I share with them what I had discovered.

Thus began the pilgrim walks which have grown in popularity over the years. Last year alone (1998) more than one hundred groups took part, consisting of a fascinating variety of people from many countries, representing young and old, Christian and non-Christian alike. From the beginning it was apparent that there is a hunger nowadays for a more natural and soulful expression of spirituality. The way of the pilgrim seems to address that need.

The Way of the Pilgrim in Glendalough Today

Pilgrimage has always been and still is an important expression of the spiritual journey. All the great religions of the world have holy places to which people feel drawn in order to find a sense of the sacred in their lives. From the time of Christ, Jerusalem has attracted pilgrims, likewise Mecca, which has the most famous pilgrimage of all. Ireland has many pilgrimage centres, including Croagh Patrick and Lough Derg, which were identified as holy places in pre-Christian times.

The journey to the sacred place was just as important as the arrival and it is the whole journey we explore in our pilgrim walks in Glendalough. The experience has a dreamlike quality and it is impossible to programme or predict what will happen. The walk takes about three hours and is circular in design, moving from the place of community represented by the Monastic City to Kevin's Desert, where the individual can find space and quiet. There are many places to stop along the way, and the ones chosen vary according to the time available and the group's own needs.

Gathering and Transition

When we first meet, people introduce themselves and share a little of where they have come from and what they are looking for. Standing together in an open space at the beginning of a pilgrim journey, it becomes clear that each person's authentic truth is their own story.

Here we take some time to make the transition from the busy world which people have just left to the more relaxed atmosphere and natural beauty of Glendalough. We set out to walk with awareness, remembering we are guests and guardians of the earth.

An old Irish prayer asks God to bless every step of the way and the soft ground beneath our feet:

> '*A Dhia, beannaigh gach chéim a bhfuil mé ag dul agus beannaigh dom an chré atá fém' chois.*'[2] (God, bless the ground beneath my feet and every step I am taking.)

Celtic spirituality had a deep sense of the mystery and presence of God in everything and everyone.

Walking the Monastic City...

Walking through the ruins of the monastic city is like a journey through time and space. The stones of the cathedral church hold the memories of prayer and worship poured forth by night and day for centuries. The round tower stands intact after a thousand years and is a magnificent symbol of faith, determination, welcome, guardianship and safety. Its seven storeys are a beautiful expression of the seven stages of human life. The four windows looking out from its top floor are like watchful eyes, observing and including every direction and road that we travel.

The model of the old monastery was that of a circle within a circle. The inner circle contained the main church, the burial ground for the dead, the abbot's house and the *prionn teach* (refectory), where guests were offered hospitality. The outer circle covered a large area on which houses were built to accommodate the whole community. The circles were joined together at the entrance or gateway from which a passage led directly to the heart of the monastery. In Celtic tradition the transition into a sacred place was always marked by a passage linking the outer and the inner, the sacred and the secular, this world and the Otherworld.

Community life in this monastic city was inclusive and contained a mixture of families, monks and visitors. It is still known locally as the Seven Churches. Six of the churches were quite small and situated within the outer enclosure. Nobody knows now what they were used for but it is likely they accommodated various small groups. It is a model of small Christian communities finding an identity within a larger organisation, which has a lot to offer the times we are living in.

Stopping by Kevin's Well...

Leaving the place of community, we sometimes visit Kevin's Well, which is located in a secluded place near the Glendasan river, not far from the monastic enclosure. There was an ancient belief that all wells had their source in one great well deep inside the centre of the earth. They were sacred places, guarded by protective feminine spirits. Water is a wonderful symbol of life. It flows in rivers and lies silently in wells and can help us get in touch with our inner life-force and deepest sources. A visit to a well can be a calming, cleansing and healing experience. Kevin's Well is encircled by a little mound of earth, with a birch tree growing at the opening. Pilgrims traditionally tied little pieces of cloth to the branches as a hope or prayer of intention, and in that way left a memory of themselves behind.

Along the Green Road...

We then continue our pilgrim journey along the Green Road towards Kevin's Desert in the inner valley. The mood of the group often changes at this point and people quite spontaneously become quieter and more reflective. A little ritual by the shore of Loch na Péist (the Lake of the Monster) is always moving and profound. Cold water is held gently in the cup of the hands and allowed to drip slowly through the fingers back into the lake. This is to symbolise holding and acknowledging the hurts, disappointment and frustration we all carry, but it is also an invitation to release them little by little. The last drops of water tend to stay within the hands, reminding us that while there may still be issues to be resolved, we have the choice to let them go. So it is with our inner pain; new possibilities in life can open up when old wounds, anger and bitterness are understood with compassion, but not allowed to control us. Perhaps then we are freer to respond to life rather than react against it.

Into Kevin's Desert...

The time spent in Kevin's Desert on the shores of the upper lake is the high point of the whole experience. Where the land meets water, there is no option but to stop, look, listen and be still. The lake stretches out before us, constantly reflecting the changing moods of life. Sometimes it is calm and peaceful, at other times dark and restless, and often wild and dangerous. Above Kevin's Bed the cliffs rise vertically, majestic and awe-inspiring, connecting earth and sky, and pointing to possibilities not yet realised. The two sides of the valley, which represent the bright and dark side of human experience, come together naturally before our eyes.

This is a place to linger for a while, looking back on the way we have travelled. Just to be there is a blessing. A gift of solitude is to remember what has been with gratitude – be present to the moment and yet open to the future. It is a tolerant and open way of being that can offer great peace. A short climb by the waterfall leads eventually to Kevin's Cell, where it is possible to sit for a while on the foundation stones of his sixth-century house. Here the scenery and the silence create an atmosphere that seems to whisper 'Be still and know thyself'. The fruit of solitude is being connected to a quiet place within ourselves, wherever we are.

On the north side of the lake, along the Miners' Road, there is a clear view of Kevin's bed, which is a rock-tomb from the Bronze Age – a thousand years before the time of Christ. There Kevin and many others down through the years spent long hours and whole nights in prayer. From the vantage point of a rock on the opposite shore, it seems near and yet beyond reach, representing the mystery and challenge of all the places we have never been. It suggests that those who lived there trusted and honoured their inner voice.

Completing the Round...

The circle or round of the pilgrim journey in Glendalough is completed by taking the main road back to the site of the old monastery. It is the brighter side of the valley where people live and the road to reconnection with the world of others. The first church reached on that side is St Mary's, also called *Teampall na mBan* (the Church of the Women). Here the atmosphere is quiet and peaceful, with a hint of sadness.

In May, the month of Mary, birds sing beautifully in the surrounding trees and primroses and bluebells flower profusely on the ground around the grave of the unbaptised children. Many tears are shed for the unfeeling attitude that condemned little children to Limbo and also for that which is marginalised within each one of us – the hopes and dreams that are never realised.

A Eucharistic Celebration...

During some pilgrim walks we include a celebration of the Eucharist. Like an Emmaus walk, stories are told and the Word of God is spoken along the road. The bread and wine are offered, blessed and shared, either on the shores of the upper lake or in one of the old churches.

Sometimes only the Liturgy of the Word is shared during the pilgrimage, while the Liturgy of the Eucharist is celebrated around a table back in my house. Invariably this leads on to a time of conversation and sharing, which includes memories of the pilgrimage just completed. It is a beautiful and blessed way to end the day.

Sacred Space

Gradually over the years, more and more people have wanted to stay, for a while, to explore for themselves the spirit of the valley and of the pilgrimage. As each of the apartments in the house has become available, I have rented them to provide accommodation. Each apartment has a name – *Dóchas* (Hope), *Cairdeas* (Friendship), *Cúinas* (Quietness) and *Sonas* (Happiness). These names express something of the longing of people when they come to stay. Because the house has emerged out of a need rather than a plan, it has a special atmosphere of its own and has become the heart of my work in Glendalough.

Our Sacred Journey

It has been said that as we let our light shine, we unconsciously give other people permission to do the same. As I have shared the realisation of my dream, others coming here have been encouraged to express their deepest longings too. Each and every person is a source of inspiration and part of my hope for the future. The way I live is only one expression of a desire at the heart of modern men and women for freedom, authenticity and spirituality in their daily lives. All I try to offer is a quiet space to be oneself, a listening and sympathetic ear, and the conviction that wherever we have come from and whoever we are, every step along the road we have travelled is an integral part of our sacred journey.

(*Written in collaboration with Gill McCarthy*)

KILDARE TODAY: CONTINUING THE BRIGIDINE TRADITION

Mary Minehan

Kildare – legendary name
The place of sanctuary,
Where Brigid found her heaven,
And the wind is whispering from the past.[1]

Cill Dara, the Gaelic name for Kildare, which means the cell or church of the oak is, in a sense, synonymous with St Brigid.[2] It is safe to say that without Brigid there would be no modern town of Kildare.[3] As the local saying goes 'All Roads Lead to Kildare'. In fact, twelve roads intersect in the town, indicating its popularity as a place of pilgrimage in earlier days. Each road converges on the ancient monastic site of St Brigid. Founded over fifteen hundred years ago, Brigid's monastery was acclaimed as a centre of education, art and worship in Ireland and far beyond it up to the suppression of the monasteries in the sixteenth century.

The Sisterhood of St Brigid

The Sisterhood of Saint Brigid was founded by Daniel Delany, Bishop of Kildare and Leighlin, in Tullow, County Carlow, in 1807. The Brigidine Annals record that Bishop Delany insisted that he was not founding a new congregation but, rather, re-founding the ancient order of the Sisters of St Brigid. As if to show the continuity between the old and the new, the Annals also record that the bishop brought an oak sapling from Kildare and planted it in the convent grounds in Tullow. A mighty oak tree in the grounds today bears testimony to this anecdote.

Returning to our Roots

In 1992 the Sisters of St Brigid took a discerned decision to return to Kildare. This return could be viewed as part of a worldwide resurgence of interest in Brigid and in all aspects of Celtic spirituality. As Brigidines, we were challenged to create a new grafting of the oak, to reclaim 'Brigid of Kildare' in a new way for a new millennium.

> The Sisters of St Brigid could help us to develop and understand the spirituality of their patroness. Their developing commitment to the issues of Justice and Peace and to the building of a more humane and caring world, should have as their origin, a distinctly Brigidine expression. Just as many Irish people over the centuries have made relevant pilgrimages to places associated with her, the Brigidine Sisters must not be backward in humbly drawing inspiration from the deep well of Brigid.[4]

We set out on a journey to walk in the footsteps of Brigid and to reconnect with our ancient Celtic heritage. We hoped that what we would experience and discover on the journey could be a life-giving pathway to the future, remembering the words of Scripture: 'I have come that you may have life and have it to the full' (John 10:10).

Kildare – A Heritage Town

Kildare town, situated about thirty miles south of Dublin, has a growing population of approximately 6,000 inhabitants. Even approaching the town from a distance, one is invited to contemplate its historic past. Many ecclesiastical establishments, former civic and political buildings, the ruins of some ancient abbeys, including a magnificent cathedral and round tower, enhance its landscape and exude a sense of sacred presence and timelessness.

The landscape is filled with echoes and memories of its founding saint. The 'Curragh', formerly known locally as 'St Brigid's Pastures', is associated with a popular legend of Brigid and boasts some of the best gallops in the world.[5] The town is the home of the Irish National Stud and welcomes over 140,000 visitors annually to view its thriving horse industry.

St Brigid's Cathedral, a thirteenth-century building, stands on an ancient monastic site known as the 'Hill of Kildare'. It has recently been restored and refurbished, and the Church of Ireland and Friends of the Cathedral can justifiably be proud of their successful achievement. Nothing remains of the original foundation, which was probably constructed of timber, mud and wattle and rebuilt many times, as the double monastery for men and women grew in numbers. In his Life of St Brigid, Cogitosus (*circa* AD 650) gives a description of a remarkable building in Kildare at that time.[6]

Beside the cathedral stands the restored foundations of 'St Brigid's Fire House', which is remembered today in a Kildare street name: Fire House Lane. Some scholars note that since pre-Christian times, priestesses met on the Hill of Kildare to light their ritual fires and to pray, invoking the pastoral goddess, Brigit, for good herds and crops. Folk tradition informs us that St Brigid retained the ritual of keeping the fire burning, and that it was kept alight by the nuns as a symbol of faith, warmth and hospitality until it was extinguished in the sixteenth century. Giraldus Cambrensis (Gerald of Wales), who visited Kildare in the thirteenth century, gives a description of the Fire House and records that the fire was so carefully tended by the nuns that it had burned constantly since Brigid's own time.[7]

Bride Street runs from the town centre to St Brigid's Church, which was very fittingly modernised following the Second

Vatican Council. The main door of the church, designed by the sculptor Imogen Stuart, is made in bronze and inlaid with St Brigid's Crosses. Its handles are suggestive of St Brigid's hospitality, as they are in the form of hands outstretched in welcome. The persistent efforts of local historians and schools to achieve heritage status for Kildare town bore fruit in having Kildare designated as a Heritage Town in 1994.

Solas Bríde (Brigid's Light)

The title of the song 'You couldn't have come at a better time'[8] is an apt commentary on our experience as Brigidine Sisters since coming to Kildare in 1992. So much has been happening and continues to happen in honour of the spirit and traditions of Brigid!

Having lived in temporary accommodation for a few years, we moved to a permanent home, *Solas Bríde* (Brigid's Light) at 14, Dara Park. It is now a small Christian community centre for Celtic Spirituality in the spirit of Brigid of Kildare. An outreach community of women and men who call themselves *Cáirde Bríde* (Friends of Brigid) has developed around the Solas Bríde community. Their vision statement reads:

> *Cáirde Bríde*, in association with the Brigidine Sisters, is a group inspired by the values of Brigid to promote peace, justice and reconciliation.

The group meets formally once a month and informally more often with the Solas Bríde community.

Kildare as a Place of Pilgrimage Today

Many tourists come to Kildare and appreciate its rich heritage. In more recent times, increasing numbers come as pilgrims and ask to be accompanied by us on their pilgrimage. The time spent with pilgrims usually includes performing a ritual at St Brigid's Well.

Pilgrims come for a variety of reasons. Some pilgrims come to find out more about St Brigid and are mystified when they hear about the pre-Christian goddess Brigid. Some come in search of the goddess and are equally mystified when they discover Brigid the saint. As scholars state, the two are inextricably interlinked.

Some pilgrims come because they belong to a parish called St Brigid's or they have attended a St Brigid's school. They come because someone in the family is or was called Brigid. They come searching for a spirituality that will nourish their lives. They come because they are interested in caring for the environment, and Brigid was a woman who had respect and reverence for the land. They come because they are interested in equality between men and women, and Brigid was a leader in the Church and society of her day. They come because they are interested in justice issues of all kinds.

Pilgrims From All Over The World

Pilgrims come from all over the world but mainly from Germany, Italy, England, Wales, Australia, New Zealand and the USA. One group of twenty-five women came from Tonsberg, Norway, for a four-day pilgrimage. They had a fascinating story to tell; they are members of *Losje Kildare* (Lodge Kildare) in Tonsberg and they call themselves *Birgitta Søstre* (Brigid's Sisters). Their association was founded in Tönsberg in 1984 and there are now approximately eight hundred Birgitta Søstre throughout Scandinavia. Membership includes married and single women. Most of the members belong to the Lutheran tradition. Brigid of Kildare is their model and they try to live her values. They meet twice a month in their lodges for a ritual incorporating reflection, silence and music, concluding with a meal and a bring-and-buy sale – the proceeds of which go to different charities. These are women who have empowered themselves by coming together under the 'Cloak of Brigid'. They continue to link with Solas Bríde.

Kildare Links with Drumcree, County Armagh

'Brigid is the woman who, above all others, embodies the spirit of pre-Christian and Christian Ireland.'[9] All Christian traditions honour her. She was pre-Reformation. Brigid's life inspires unity and reconciliation. Discovering that Kildare was called Drumcree (i.e. 'the Ridge of Clay') prior to Brigid's foundation, has been significant.[10] Contact has been made with people of different religious traditions in Drumcree, Portadown, County Armagh, and mutual exchange visits have taken place. It is interesting, too, to discover that a new housing estate in Kildare has been called Drumcree Court.

Re-Lighting Brigid's Fire

Contemporaneously with our return to Kildare, AFRI (Action from Ireland), a renowned justice, peace and human rights group based in Dublin, was planning to celebrate the tenth anniversary of its 'St Brigid's Peace Cross Project'.[11] AFRI decided to mark this anniversary with a Peace and Justice Conference entitled 'Brigid: Prophetess, Earthwoman and Peacemaker'. Kildare town was chosen as the venue and AFRI invited us to take part in the planning at local level.

It certainly was a conference with a difference! It commenced with more than twenty young pilgrims, who bore a lighted flame, walking thirty-six miles from the valley of Glendalough in County Wicklow to Kildare. On their arrival in the town, 'St Brigid's fire or flame' was symbolically re-lit in the Town Square by Mary Teresa Cullen, the then Congregational Leader of the Sisters of St Brigid. It was an historic and poignant moment for the 250 participants – the flame burned in the Town Square for the duration of the conference.

At the conference, a panel of well-known speakers from Ireland, England, New Zealand and the US spoke on major justice and human rights issues facing today's world. A columnist in a national daily newspaper remarked when writing about the conference:

> No better model than Brigid could be found for a symposium on the evils of poverty, injustice, inequality and war.[12]

Ritual and Legend

In the meaningful and varied rituals throughout the conference there was an imaginative and innovative use of fire, water, clay, bread, fruit, mime and dance. These were performed in the churches and at St Brigid's Well. Some Brigidine legends and myths were dramatised and re-told as parables, and their implications for today's world were vividly illustrated. One legend, for example, that speaks to people, tells of Brigid's extraordinary compassion and concern for the poor. For her, Christ was seen in every person, especially in the guise of the poor person. It goes:

> One day when Brigid was on a long journey she stopped to rest by the wayside. A wealthy lady, on hearing that Brigid was in the neighbourhood, brought her a beautiful basket of choice apples. No sooner had the gift been presented than a group of poor people came by and begged for food. Without hesitation Brigid distributed to them the choice apples. The donor was utterly disgusted and said to Brigid: 'I brought those apples for you, not for them'. Brigid's reply was: 'What is mine is theirs'.[13]

What are the implications of this legend for us as citizens of Ireland and of the world today? A world where 25% of the earth's population own and consume 75% of the world's resources? What does this legend call us to do in terms of the need to work for a fairer distribution of the wealth being generated in our Celtic Tiger economy? One of the major issues confronting us is a widening poverty gap, as the rich get richer and the poor grow poorer. Individuals and groups concerned with justice issues can draw inspiration from Brigid's sense of justice, which inspired her to take the initiative and say 'What's mine is theirs'.

Before the conference concluded, it was suggested that Brigid's flame, having been re-lit, should be kept alight. We are honoured to be the keepers of the flame in Solas Bríde. It is our hope that the flame will be perpetually re-lit and restored to its true home in Brigid's Fire House during the forthcoming millennium celebrations.

From the Curragh to the Great Wall!

The re-lighting of Brigit's flame seems to have caught the imagination of people worldwide and it has been symbolically brought to many countries since it has been re-lit. Nóirín Ní Ríain, international spiritual singer and songwriter, carried the flame to China, to the fourth United Nations' Women's Conference in Beijing. We, together with some members of Cáirde Bríde, were privileged to accompany her as far as the Royal Festival Hall in London, where we were invited to open a rock concert for over 2,000 participants with a ritual incorporating the flame and the weaving of a St Brigid's Cross, into which was woven some of the hopes and aspirations of the women of the world. Nóirín tells the rest of the story in her own inimitable style:

What a symbol of ongoing female strength and spirituality! ...How could I carry a naked flame, a burning candle half way across the world? ...I carried the flame aboard the plane in a charcoal handwarmer that lasted eight hours until I got to Moscow; I then re-kindled from this stick another which lasted right into China! All I can say here, friends, in the light of my experience of carrying Brigid's light, is that she is a trickster and loved kicking her heels in style from the Curragh to the Great Wall.[14]

Féile Bríde – An Annual Spring-time Conference and Festival

From this two-day conference on Brigid in 1993 has evolved what is now known as *Féile Bríde* (The Festival of Brigid). In one sense it is a revival of what was once an ancient Celtic festival called *Imbolc*. Our early ancestors danced like children to the mystery of new life and sprouting vegetation at this Festival of Imbolc and they lit great fires to banish the tired spirits of winter and darkness. Féile Bríde is now a four-day event, with a Justice and Peace Conference as a core component. It is a holistic festival in the sense that the secular and the sacred are intertwined. Brigid's God was one who delighted in life, in feasting and dancing. How else can we explain her description of heaven as 'a Great Lake of Beer'![15] Brigid, as patroness of poets, artisans and healing, attracts an array of poets and artists to the festival; they come to find inspiration and to drink from the deep ancestral wellspring of Brigid.

The Féile is not just a 'once off' event that happens for four days and then all is over until February (springtime) comes around again. We, with Cáirde Bríde, marvel at the amount of action and interaction that takes place after the festival is over, arising from the issues discussed at the Peace and Justice Conference. We marvel, too, at the links and bonds that are forged throughout the festival and at the interconnectedness that continues the process of keeping the flame enkindled throughout the year.

Conclusion

This chapter gives a flavour of some of the happenings in Kildare today. As we approach the new millennium, Brigid is emerging as one whose values can nourish life in all of creation. Many people are in search of a spirituality that emphasises the immanence, the closeness of God, and connects all of life. Brigid cultivated such a spirituality in her own life. Creativity, love and hope abound in Kildare today as we try to unravel and weave anew the threads of Brigid's cloak and life.

> We have only begun to imagine the fullness of life,
> How could we tire of hope?
> so much is in bud,
> so much is unfolding that must complete its gesture,
> so much is in bud.[16]

CELTIC HOLINESS AND
MODERN ECO-WARRIORS

Nuala Ahern

The separation of mind and nature, of sexuality and spirituality, of male and female, is a fundamental crisis of our world. This dualistic separation has given our civilisation its force and power but it now threatens the survival of life itself. An industrial society, which began as an enlightened system intended for progress and development, leads us towards planetary destruction. It has created the accelerating decimation of the planet's diversity of species and human cultures. Now our scientific culture even proposes the termination of nature's fertility – suicide seeds that are genetically engineered to self-destruct rather than regenerate. This is a shocking symbol of the death of nature wrought by human technology.

Christianity in early Ireland kept the tradition of the holiness of nature, which it had inherited from the pre-Christian Irish tradition. Pelagius, the Irish contemporary of St Patrick, taught the incorruptibility of nature, and Duns Scotus Eriugena held that the living body of Christ is the world, not the Church, for God is in all things....[1]

This Irish spiritual tradition was subversive to the alienation of spirit and nature, for in it we find a holistic, ecological world view which held that there was a force or spirit that moves through all living things, giving them life and strength. Trees, sacred mounds, groves, springs, rivers, lakes and wells, were the focal points of this energy, which was immanent in the land. Celtic religious tradition was and still is bound up with the sanctity of the land and the power of the holy place and shrine.

Neart (Power)

Spirit was deemed to be an active force, as expressed in the Irish word *neart.* This suggests passion, vivacity, excitement, sexuality, inspiration, blazing energy, tumultuous fury, speed, heat and light. Poets, saints and heroes are filled with *neart.* The holy one is one who is filled with this strength. The ancient words to describe the hero or warrior express the same idea. *Nia,* for example, symbolised warlike passion, vivacity, energy, excitement and holiness – holiness was originally regarded as an active force.

It was important to connect with this source of spiritual strength through visiting the holy places at sacred times of the year. At the time of the great Celtic festivals, it was believed that the Otherworld broke through everywhere into this world, but most especially at the sacred places of the earth. Rites and rituals were necessary both to protect the people from the malignant aspects of the Otherworld, and to avail of its benign aspects of healing and plenty.

The Celtic Otherworld

The Celtic Otherworld is the place of timelessness and of eternity – but it is not sealed off or a place apart. It was possible to visit the Otherworld, to have visions and experiences of it in this life, and emerge transformed and reborn. St Patrick therefore in the Irish tradition could descend into hell and return renewed, healed and filled with *neart.*

The ways of travelling to the Otherworld are through music or the recitation of poetry, through dream, vision, story, prayer or fasting, through a voyage over the sea or across a lake, or through entering a cave or drinking from the 'well of life'.

A Psychological rather than an Historical Focus

A crucial aspect of the Irish spiritual tradition which underlies the Otherworld 'experience' is that religious thought is expressed not historically but psychologically. The attention is on the meaning that a particular story or event has. It becomes part of the present in some way, affects life in the here and now, is re-presented or re-told rather than fixed forever in the past. Irish mythology therefore tells us, not of miracles long past, but of the miraculous potential within ourselves, here, now and forever.

This strong psychological rather than historical focus of the pre-Christian Celtic tradition lent to Christian spirituality in Ireland the power of experience as well as of faith. One did not have to wait for miracles or wonders until the end of time, but rather, through an engagement with the timeless Otherworld, one could evoke the visions and gifts of the spirit in this world. The early medieval pilgrimage to St Patrick's Purgatory on Lough Derg originally allowed the pilgrim an imitation of the saint's descent into hell and his rebirth into this world – renewed, having fasted for nine days, returning with gifts of healing and transformation.

The Celtic Festivals – The Wheel Of The Year

The unifying force over the whole of the Celtic world was the celebration of the festivals, which constituted the wheel of the year. The wheel of the year was the axis on which the world turned, an interaction between sacred place and sacred time. The cyclical nature of the universe, and the death and rebirth that maintained this great cycle, were celebrated at the four major festivals or quarter days. These were *Samhain* (Halloween), *Féile Bríde* (St Brigit's Day), *Bealtaine* (Mayday), and *Lughnasa* (Harvest's Beginning).[2]

Samhain (Halloween, 31 October/1 November) was the time of the descent of winter, the turn of the year towards darkness and death. This was the time when the festival of the dead was held, when the spirits of the ancestors were venerated and when they could communicate with the living. Fires were lit against the encroaching darkness and the fruits of the harvest were enjoyed in games and celebration. We celebrate it today as Halloween, and the Feast of All Saints and All Souls, when each family remembers its dead. The festival survives as Remembrance Day across Europe.

Féile Bríde (The Festival of Brigit, 31 January/1 February) celebrated the loosening of winter's grip, the beginning of spring, the return of light and life after darkness, cold and death, when Brigit tiptoed across the land, warming it as she passed. Weddings were celebrated around this time, with customs which are now displaced to Valentine's Day and leap year. Many healing traditions invoke the protection of Brigit over the family and over the safety of livestock, particularly the safe birthing of lambs, which takes place at this time.

Bealtaine (May Eve/Day) celebrated the beginning of summer's generativity. It was traditionally celebrated by fires, dancing and rituals encouraging fertility. Now celebrated as Labour Day, May Day survives as a 'festival of the people' throughout Europe into the twenty-first century.

The Festival of *Lughnasa* (not fixed) was the festival of first fruits at the beginning of harvest – celebrated during the last week in July and the first week of August. Processions or excursions to hills in one's own locality formed the main feature of the celebration. Wild berries, just ripening, were customarily picked and eaten. There were also larger communal gatherings, among them the ascent of Croagh Patrick, one of Ireland's greatest penitential pilgrimages, in which many people still participate to the present day.

There are many traditions about the first crop of potatoes or the first cut of the corn at Lughnasa. Stories were told of the conflict of bloom and blight over the harvest. Singing, dancing and the racing of horses across water also occurred and continues in some areas today. Fairs were held, among them survivals such as the Old Lammas fair at Ballycastle, County Antrim.

Value of Festive Celebration for Community

The celebration of the Celtic festivals maintained the Celtic tradition of harmony between time and timelessness and the closeness and accessibility of the Otherworld. Communal celebration in music, dance, prayer, song and intoxication, allowed for the experience of the timelessness of the Otherworld through complete participation in this world. The story of the origin of the sacred told at the sacred time, the practice of pilgrimage in circular ritual, the practice of penitence, the whirling patterns of dance, the chanting of prayer, the singing of songs, brought the participants the experience of renewal.

Renewal was also experienced by celebrating in tandem with the cycle of natural life. The death of the natural world is followed by rebirth and renewal, and a spiritual engagement with this brings a cyclical sense of renewal to the individual and community. Participation in the renewal of the natural world allows a mystical experience of the sacred through engagement with this world. The divine power in nature evokes spiritual rebirth.

These occasions were marked at the sacred places of the locality. Each locality had its own sacred hill or mound, holy well, bush or tree located near a shrine. Spirituality, therefore, was firmly rooted in local attachment to place. The strong sense of the continuity of the natural world, combined with the strong sense of place, helped the community to connect in right relationship with the living world around them. These festivals, therefore, and the later Christian festivals of Easter, Christmas, Whitsun, Pentecost, holy days and feast days, gave structure to the community.

Relevance Today

The tradition I have been describing is one which acknowledged in its story and rituals divine immanence. How can this kind of consciousness help us today? If in Celtic tradition the source of the Otherworldy experience is firmly rooted in the natural world, then, should we not be witnessing to the sanctity of land, sea, ocean, lakes, rivers? Can our Celtic tradition help us realise the need to save the life of a tree as we would that of a person, and should we not see the destruction of even one as a terrible crime? One example of those who have answered the call to witness to the sanctity of the land are the eco-warriors.

Eco-Warriors 'Glen Vigil', County Wicklow – A Spiritual Battle

The vigil of the eco-warriors in the Glen of the Downs, County Wicklow, during the final years of the twentieth century, is a spiritual offensive against the global destruction of our species. They are peaceful warriors, mostly young, dug in for the long haul. They arrived seemingly from nowhere. A few letters in *The Irish Times*, a piece on the Internet: the story of an oak glen under threat went all over the world, and the tree-warriors arrived to save it.

The tree-warriors do not live in the pragmatic world of compromise but have taken an Otherworld journey in space and time – to do spiritual battle. To the tree-warriors it does not matter if it is 2% or 4% of the trees that will be cut. They do not think in percentages, but about eco-systems, about the life that is an oak tree. The tree has a spirit and must not be cut. When a tree is cut down, they wail in grief and despair.

Their despair takes on an even greater significance when we remind ourselves that the Oak, along with the Ash and Hazel, was one of the most sacred trees in the Celtic tradition, being connected to many ancient Holy Places of significance in Ireland, such as Doire (Derry) and Cill Dara (Kildare).

The tree-warriors hold sacred vigils resembling the sacred vigils held in marking our Celtic Festivals. Visiting them on a Sunday afternoon is like a saint's holy day or a pilgrimage revived. There is a holy well hung with woven symbols. There are trees hung with prayer rags. There is a bender with a fire and musicians and singers. There is a throng of well-wishers come to pay their respects to what is an ancient tradition – a kind of penitential life in the service of a cause.

A Penitential Life on Behalf of the Community

The penitence of the eco-warriors is performed on behalf of the whole community. Their outer-inner journey represents a journey that we all must make if the planet is to survive. A return to a philosophy that truly reveres the material world as sacred is needed as we enter the third millennium. The world may seem boundless, endless and enduring, but it has proved fragile against the onslaught of an unsustainable way of life. Can we learn to enjoy the abundance of the world without gobbling it up in our greed?

How should we proceed? How does this view of the land as sacred fit with a utilitarian model of the world, or even within a framework of sustainable development or negotiation and conflict resolution? And how do we turn direct action from conflict to prayer?

We can proceed: by always keeping to the path of non-violence; by standing over all our actions as a witness in saying who we are and what we stand for; by never taking covert action or using denial or collusion in actions that are covert; and by taking our action in the knowledge of the whole community. The support we lend to individuals and groups such as the eco-warriors is a true embracing of the holiness of our Celtic Spirituality!

THE SÍOL RETREAT: A CELTIC
CELEBRATION IN AN IGNATIAN SETTING

Fionnuala Ní Chuill

Luím ar mo leaba mar a luífinn san uaigh;
deinim m'fhaoistin go crua leat, a Dhia.
A Íosa, caithfead bás d'fháil.
Ní heol dom conas ná cathain ná canad.
Ach dá bhfaighinn bás i bpeaca marfach,
bheadh m'anam caillte go deo.
A Íosa, dein trócaire orm,
A Íosa, dein trua agus taise dhom,
A Íosa, tabhair cabhair agus cúnamh dom. Amen.

I lie on my bed as I would lie in the grave;
I confess sincerely to you, O God.
Jesus, I must die.
I know not how or when or where.
But if I were to die in mortal sin,
I would be lost forever.
Jesus, have mercy on me,
Jesus, have pity and compassion on me,
Jesus, come to my aid and help me. Amen.

The above prayer brings back one of my earliest memories –
that of my father doing the round of the bedrooms each night
as we children lay in our beds ready for sleep. Having recited
the prayer, my father then raised his hand in true pontifical
fashion and blessed each one of us individually '*in ainm an
Athar agus an Mhic agus an Spioraid Naoimh*' (In the name of
the Father and of the Son and of the Holy Spirit). This nightly
ritual – a prayer for a particular occasion, followed by a

Trinitarian blessing – was my introduction to Celtic prayer and spirituality.

I was introduced to 'The Exercises of St Ignatius' through the preached retreats of my novitiate days. The Ignatian-directed retreats of post Vatican Two days taught me to pray Scripture (as opposed to interpreting it). Some years later, in far-off Washington State, I chose to study St Patrick's 'Confession' and wrote a mini-thesis on his spirituality. In doing so, I realised that I had come across the roots of our Celtic spirituality in Patrick's love of the Word of God and in his mystical relationship with the Trinity. When I later came to adapting the Exercises, with the help of the late Sr Marie Rene, I saw the benefit of weaving our own Celtic spirituality into the Ignatian framework. The result was the Síol Retreat, which started in Ireland in June 1984.

My purpose in writing this article is to illustrate how the Ignatian and Celtic spiritualities share a common core element, which made their fusion in the Síol Retreat a harmonious blend. The goal of the Exercises, which is 'Finding God in All Things', is very closely related to the 'Sense of Divine Presence' which is at the heart of Celtic spirituality. I will first explain these two core elements and then follow, with a more detailed look at the implication of 'Presence' in that unique spiritual heritage of ours usually referred to as Celtic Spirituality.

The Exercises of St Ignatius; Finding God in All Things

The Ignatian Exercises could be described as a thirty-day or a four-week prayer programme devised by St Ignatius. It is written in the form of paragraphs called annotations, some of which have titles and all of which are numbered. For my purposes here, I will deal only with *The Foundation: Fact and Practice* (23) and with *The Contemplatio ad Amorem*, otherwise known as *The Contemplation Towards Love* (234-237).

The Foundation clearly states that the purpose of our existence is union with God. All God's gifts are there to lead us towards that end: we use them in so far as they help us towards union and we let go of them if they prove a hindrance to union. In the Exercises, therefore, we journey in prayer towards intimacy with the Trinity. The Foundation precedes the Contemplatio, and what may seem like a duty (in the Foundation) becomes permeated and illuminated with love in the Contemplatio.

In the Contemplatio, Ignatius invites me as an individual to contemplate God as the giver and source of all love and of all gift. I am asked to become aware of the various manifestations of God's love in my life and in the world around me and to respond as I ought.

I contemplate how God first loved me; how I was created out of gratuitous love; how God gifted me with the many tokens of his love scattered throughout the universe; how God chooses to dwell within me; and how God labours to share his life and love with me.

Ignatius challenges me to contemplate all this for a purpose i.e. in order that I would Find God in All Things, and make a fitting response. He encourages me to respond generously to such boundless, extravagant love and gives me what is generally known as the 'Suscipe' prayer to help me:

> Take, Lord, and receive all my liberty,
> my memory, my understanding, and my entire will –
> all that I have and call my own.
> You have given it all to me.
> To you, Lord, I return it.
> Everything is yours; do with it what you will.
> Give me only your love and your grace.
> That is enough for me (234).

Celtic Spirituality: A Celebration of Presence

The Celtic Spirituality of Presence, in which God is perceived as an indwelling and intimate God, immanent and yet transcendent, ever-present to our daily situations, is closely related to the experience of the Contemplatio. Although older by more than a thousand years, Celtic spirituality, in its beginnings, answers to the upper reaches of the Exercises as exemplified in the Contemplatio. In other words, Celtic spirituality springs from where the Exercises of St Ignatius end. There is only one explanation for this – a great number of our early Irish saints and their followers were mystics, like St Patrick before them.

A Spirituality of the Senses – Exterior and Interior

These saints not only believed in the loving indwelling of the Godhead in themselves and in all created things, they also experienced the Divine Presence through their inner senses. They even talked of ten senses – five exterior and five interior. In explaining and in passing on the mystery of God's presence in our world, these saints passed on more than dry dogma because they knew more than dry dogma – they knew what they were talking about at an experiential level. This was, as An tAthair Donnchadh Ó Floinn has described it, 'a breathing in and a breathing out of God'.

It was out of this collective peak experience of God's immanence that Irish/Celtic spirituality emerged to infuse every aspect and every dimension of daily living. This was an outdoor spirituality staged in the theatre of God's universe and tuned to the rhythms of nature; it was an indoor spirituality which took account of the needs and chores of women and children as well as of men; it was a personal spirituality which challenged the individual to intimacy and discipleship; it was a community spirituality which stemmed from a deep understanding of the

Mystical Body of Christ; it was an exultant spirituality which recognised the harmony and connectedness of all things.

Having found God in all things, the Celt celebrated this discovery in prayer, poetry and practice for centuries to come and in a diluted fashion down to the present day.

I have explored the Celtic Awareness of Divine Presence under three main themes: a) Divine Awareness in Creation, b) Divine Awareness in People, and c) Divine Awareness in Everyday Life Situations.

(a) Celtic Awareness of Divine Presence in Creation

The Celts read creation as we read books. Creation, in all its beauty and fury, was for them a revelation of the Godhead. 'If you want to know the Creator, understand created things', St Columbanus taught. This is reminiscent of St Patrick's response to Etne Alba, when she, a Celtic princess, asks him:

> Who is God?... Where is His dwelling?... In the seas, in the rivers, in the mountains, in the valleys?...

and he replies:

> Our God, God of all men,
> God of heaven and earth, seas and rivers,
> god of sun and moon, of all the stars,
> God of high mountains and of lowly valleys,
> God over heaven, and in heaven, and under heaven.
> He has a dwelling in heaven and earth and sea
> and in all things that are in them.
> He inspires all things, He quickens all things,
> He is over all things, He supports all things...[1]

The Celts renounced their numerous gods of seas, rivers, mountains and valleys for the One True God, creator of all and present in all.

Celtic Monastic Commitment to God the Creator

The Celtic hermits were single-minded in their commitment to God the Creator. They chose the most secluded but also the most beautiful places for their ascetical lifestyles. Their lives became intertwined with the rhythms of the seasons and the pace of their isolated world. Their poems tell us of the peace, tranquillity and joy that they experienced in their remote hideouts. They acknowledged with gratitude that *Rí na nDúl* (the King of the Elements) had supplied them with all their basic needs – food, water and shelter. Their poetry was nature poetry transformed into praise and prayer as they found God in the beauty of his creation. The following early poem called 'The Lark', translated by Robin Flower, is a fine example of this tradition:

> Learned in music Sings the lark,
> I leave my cell to listen;
> His open beak spills music, hark!
> Where Heavens bright cloudlets glisten
>
> And so I will sing my morning psalm
> That God bright Heaven may give me
> And keep me in eternal calm
> And from all sin relieve me.[2]

God and His Creation in Modern Irish Poetry

In more recent times, Irish poets writing in both Irish and English are still inspired by the Presence of God in his creation. History, however, particularly the experience of Penal Days and Famine Times, has coloured much of this type of religious nature poetry, emphasising the suffering or crucified Christ. In Máirtín Ó Direáin's poem 'Crainn Oíche Sheaca' (Trees on a Frosty Night), 'each tree recalls the Passion tree, the tree of Crucifixion'.[3] Joseph Mary Plunkett, in his well-known poem 'I see His Blood upon the Rose', finds the presence of Christ reflected throughout the universe. The passion of the suffering Christ breaks through in the concluding lines: 'His crown of thorns is twined with every thorn; His cross is every tree'.[4]

In the turmoil of our modern world, the peace and tranquillity of monastic times emerges once more. The joy of finding the Presence of God in the ploughing of the brown earth moved Patrick Kavanagh to write lines such as:

> Tranquillity walks with me
> And no care.
> O, the quiet ecstasy
> Like a prayer.
>
> I find a star-lovely art
> In a dark sod.
> Joy that is timeless! O heart
> That knows God![5]

(b) Celtic Awareness of Divine Presence in People – Traditional Irish Hospitality

'Ireland of the Welcomes' is a name of which we are justly proud. Hospitality has been a particularly Irish trait since pagan times. In those days of Brehon Laws, refusal of hospitality was deemed an offence.

With the conversion from paganism, the concept of hospitality was Christianised. The text of Matthew 25 regarding the Last Judgement, 'I was hungry and you gave me to eat... etc.', was taken very seriously. The directive was lived out in a practical way by the Celtic monks and their followers. All the Celtic monasteries had a 'Teach Aíochta' or 'House of Hospitality' attached. Here, the monks supplied food, drink and overnight lodgings to all passers-by free of charge.

In the Guest or Vagrant is Christ Received

For the Celtic monk, the guest was always Christ and hospitality was offered to the Christ in the other. We have numerous illustrations of this in early Irish literature:

> If there be a guest in your house
> and you conceal aught from him,
> 'tis not the guest who will be without
> but Jesus, Mary's Son.[6]

The same generous welcome was extended to visiting monks. There is an anecdote told about St Crónán, who was unexpectedly visited by a neighbouring abbot and his retinue of monks. While they were eating at table, a young novice was heard to observe in a loud voice:

> 'I see there will be no matins celebrated in this place tonight'. To whom St Crónán said, 'Brother, in the guest is received Christ; Therefore at the coming of Christ we ought to feast and rejoice. But if you had not said that the angels of God them selves would have prayed on our behalf here this night'.[7]

Nearer our own time, the same Christian truth is restated by Joseph Campbell in his poem 'Every Shuiler is Christ' (*shuiler* meaning vagrant). The final verse reads as follows:

Then when the shuiler begs,
Be neither hard nor cold:
The share that goes for Christ
Will come a hundred-fold.[8]

Holy Family Ritually Welcomed in Homes at Christmas

It is hardly surprising to find that, in the Celtic tradition, the same open welcome was extended to the Holy Family at Christmas. We have the lovely custom of leaving the table set, the fire lit, the door on the latch and a lighted candle in the window to direct and welcome Jesus, Mary and Joseph into our homes and hearts on Christmas night. Máirtín Ó Direáin captures the idea in his poem 'Cuireadh do Mhuire' (Invitation to the Virgin) as he issues his invitation thus:

An eol duit, a Mhuire,
Cá rachair i mbliana
Ag iarraidh foscaidh
Do do Leanbh Naofa,
Tráth a bhfuil gach doras
Dúnta ina éadan
Ag fuath is uabhar
An chine dhaonna?

Deonaigh glacadh
Le cuireadh uaimse
Go hoileán mara
San Iarthar cianda:
Beidh coinnle geala
I ngach fuinneog lasta
Is tine mhóna
Ar theallach adhainte.

Dost thou know, O Mary,
Where thou wilt go this year
Seeking shelter for thy Holy child
When every door is closed in his face
By the hate and pride of the human race.
Deign to accept my invitation
To a sea-bound island in the remote west:
Shining candles will be lit in each window
And a fire of turf on each hearthstone kindled.[9]

(c) Celtic Awareness of Divine Presence in Life Situations

Celtic spirituality, as Diarmuid Ó Laoghaire claims, 'did not suffer a stiff dichotomy between the sacred and the profane'. It recognised all of life as holy. Every occasion was seen as a God-filled moment and no event was so trivial as not to contain the mystery of the Godhead.

Everyday Blessings and Greetings

In such a culture, everyday encounters became occasions of prayer when accompanied by such greetings as *'Dia is Muire dhíbh'* (God and Mary be with you) or *'Dé bhur mbeatha'* (May God be your life). Entering a room with the words *'Dia anseo isteach'* (May God enter here) drew a blessing on all within. Seeing a neighbour at work called forth a blessing on the work – *'Bail ó Dhia ar an obair'* (God bless the work).

In gratitude for receiving a drink the following was said, *'Go dtuga Dia deoch dod anam as an dtobar nach dtráfaidh go deo'* (May God give drink to your soul from the well that will never run dry). This blessing would serve equally well as a toast. There are many other such greetings and blessings in the Irish language. A notable feature of these greetings is that their form is usually in the plural as the Presence of Christ in the other is also acknowledged.

Trinitarian blessings were very common and often accompanied particular tasks. The housewife cut the Sign of the Cross into the dough as she blessed it: *'In ainm an Athar agus an Mhic agus an Spioraid Naoimh'*. When milking, the first drop of milk was used to bless the cow 'In the name of the Father and of the Son and of the Holy Spirit'. A triple Trinitarian blessing was used to bless the fire when banking it up with ashes at night – a blessing for the top, bottom and middle of the fire. This triple Trinitarian blessing was also used on the crown of the child's head after bathing the baby. With the development of modern conveniences, many of these tasks with their accompanying blessings have died out. However, the custom of blessing oneself or another with holy water when leaving or entering the house is still quite common.

Folk Prayers

Our ancestors, believing that God was with them in everything they did, were moved to address the Divine Presence in prayer as they began each new chore. No matter what the task or what the event, Celtic spirituality provides us with a prayer to suit the particular occasion. Many of these prayers have been published by the Celtic scholar Diarmuid Ó Laoghaire SJ, in his book entitled *Ár bPaidreacha Dúchais*. These are all folk prayers composed by the ordinary people and passed on orally from generation to generation. The following is one example – a prayer for dressing the bed:

> *Cóirím an leaba seo inniu*
> *in ainm an Athar, an Mhic agus an Spioraid Naoimh,*
> *in ainm na hoíche a gineadh sinn,*
> *in ainm an lae a baisteadh sinn,*
> *in ainm gach naoimh is gach aspail*
> *dá bhfuil sna Flaithis.*[10]

I dress this bed today
in the name of the Father, the Son and the Holy Spirit,
in the name of the night of our conception,
in the name of the day of our baptism,
in the name of every saint and apostle in Heaven.

A Down-to-Earth Spirituality... Relevant in Ireland Today

The sense of the Divine Presence in Creation, in people and in life situations, is at the heart of Celtic spirituality. Once experienced, one cannot but celebrate it and be moved, to some degree, to live accordingly, as our ancestors did. As John Mac Quarrie says, Celtic spirituality is 'a down-to-earth spirituality'.[11] It is a spirituality that can offer us much in the Ireland of today as we sadly pollute creation, reject the stranger and fail to acknowledge the divine in our life situations.

The Síol Retreat – Celtic Spirituality in an Ignatian Setting

The Síol Retreat is an adaptation of the Exercises of St Ignatius. While it celebrates Celtic spirituality, it also follows the pattern and in-built dynamic of the Exercises. Like the Exercises, it is Scripture-based. The Ignatian pattern is simple but powerful. Each of the four weeks of the full Exercises has its own dominant theme and key exercise(s). These are faithfully adhered to throughout the Síol Retreat.

The Ignatian journey begins by emphasising God's personal love for each one of us. This in turn leads us to repentance and reconciliation, and challenges us to discipleship. We are then introduced to the mysteries of the Life of Christ, beginning with his Incarnation and ending with his Passion, Death and Resurrection. It is the contemplation of Christ's love for us throughout his own life's journey that enables us 'to know him more clearly, to love him more dearly and to follow him more nearly'. Ignatius finally, through the Contemplatio (234-237), leads us into the awareness of the Risen Christ in our world. Finding God in all things is our faith response to the mystery of that loving Presence. This, in turn, challenges us to total surrender, as expressed in Ignatius' 'Suscipe' prayer (see above).

Success of Síol Retreat in Late-Twentieth-Century Ireland.

The Síol Retreat has been in existence since 1984. Although generally aimed at the adult Irish laity, it is a retreat for all people. Upon completion, the participants are asked what the retreat has done for them. It is exciting and rewarding to note that the great majority explain God's workings in their souls as follows:

> 'Awareness of the Presence of God is a new thing in my life'; 'I became aware of God's presence in each person'; 'My religion has been brought into everyday life'.

In a sense, these responses are not to be wondered at. After all, we have the influence of almost fifteen hundred years of Christian Celtic spirituality within us – deep within our psyche. My hope would be that what is dormant within would continue to be awakened in all retreatants and in the thousands who are still searching. The Divine Presence remains always within us and the Risen Christ continues to labour on our behalf:

> Ag Críost an síol,
> Ag Críost an fómhar,
> In iothlann Dé
> Go dtugtar sinn.
>
> Christ's is the seed,
> And Christ's is the Harvest,
> Into God's granary
> May we be drawn.[12]

CONTRIBUTORS

MARY T. CONDREN was born in Dublin, and studied at the University of Hull, Boston College and Harvard University where she graduated with a doctorate in religion, gender and culture. Her dissertation was 'The Role of Sacrifice in the Construction of a Gendered Social Order and Gendered System of Representation.' She is the author of many articles on feminist theory, spirituality and liberation theology. Her first book is *The Serpent and the Goddess: Women, Religion and Power in Celtic Ireland*, (Harper Collins, 1989). She is currently the director of the Institute for Feminism and Religion in Ireland, whose aim is 'to reclaim religion by engaging theoretically and experientially with the issues of feminist theology, ritual, spirituality and ethics.' She is a research associate in women's studies at Trinity College, Dublin where she teaches gender, religion and representation.

DOLORES WHELAN is an educator and spiritual guide who founded and co-ordinated the Iomlanú Centre for Healing and Creative Living in Dundalk, County Louth, for ten years. The focus of her work is the evocation of wholeness and the hidden potential in each person. Since 1985, she has been leading workshops in human and spiritual development. Much of her work explores the influence of the pre-Celtic and Celtic cultures and its application to the soul journey of people in today's Western culture. She has been leading tours to sacred sites in Ireland since 1990. She has spoken on Celtic spirituality at conferences in Ireland, Scotland, England, Holland and the USA. Dolores' training includes: a Masters degree in spirituality (Holynames, Oakland, California), a Masters degree in biochemistry (Trinity College, Dublin) and diplomas in psychosynthesis, counselling and massage. She is also a traditional Reiki teacher. Dolores is author of *Your Breaking Point – Stress Management* (Dublin: Attic, 1993) and is a frequent broadcaster with RTÉ.

JOHN J. Ó RÍORDÁIN is a Redemptorist missionary, born in County Cork and educated in Galway, Limerick, Seattle and Montreal. As well as giving parish missions all over Ireland and Scotland, he lectures and gives short courses in history, spirituality, theology and developmental psychology. A prolific author, his recent publications include *The Music of What Happens, Celtic Spirituality: A View from the Inside* (Dublin: Columba, 1996), *A Pilgrim in Celtic Scotland* (Columba, 1997) and *Irish Catholic Spirituality: Celtic and Roman* (Columba, 1998).

PADRAIGÍN CLANCY is a graduate in Irish folklore and history and has recently completed post-graduate study with the Department of Irish Folkore (UCD). Throughout the past decade she has lectured and facilitated retreats and seminars countrywide on Irish folklore/history and Celtic spirituality. She has appeared frequently on national and local radio and television. Among the programmes she has contributed to are RTÉ's Gay Byrne Radio Show, *The Late Late Show, Limelight, Nationwide, Open House,* TG4's *Síbín* and *Turas Anama.* In 1998 she researched and presented a radio documentary on the Strawboys (RTÉ) and in 1999 she contributed to a joint RTÉ/BBC millennium television production on the history of Irish spirituality (RTÉ, spring 2000). A native of Dublin, Padraigín spent several years living on Árainn (Inis Mór), Aran Islands, County Galway, where she made an extensive collection of island folklore. She has contributed to several publications including *The Book of Aran* (Tír Eolas, 1995) and *Sinsear; The Folklore Journal* (UCD). Her thesis topic is 'The Yearly Round in Árainn na Naomh (Aran of the Saints): Calendar Custom and Belief in an Island Community'. *Celtic Threads* is Padraigín's first edited collection and will be followed by her own publication on the Celtic calendar. She is a member of the Roman Catholic Church's Jubilee 2000 Irish Spirituality and Irish Heritage Committee and also works in an advisory capacity for the National Heritage Council. A keen tinwhistle player and Irish set-dancer, Padraigín is a member of Comhaltas Ceoltóirí Éireann.

MARCUS LOSACK is an Anglican priest who studied theology at Cambridge University and the Irish School of Ecumenics, and worked in parishes in Ireland, Britain and North Africa. He was lecturer and course director at St George's College in Jerusalem, where he regularly led pilgrimages to the ancient desert monasteries of Egypt and Sinai. He is now director of Céile Dé, an ecumenical organisation in Ireland that specialises in the development of study programmes and pilgrimages in Celtic spirituality. Marcus is co-author with Michael Rodgers of *Glendalough – A Celtic Pilgrimage* (Dublin: Columba, 1996).

SEÁN Ó DUINN is a Benedictine monk and priest of Glenstal Abbey. He lectures in Irish Heritage Studies in Mary Immaculate College, University of Limerick. His published works are *Orthaí Cosanta sa Chráifeacht Cheilteach*, a research work on the 'Protection Prayer' tradition (Maigh Nuad, 1990), and a new edition of the ancient Irish saga: *Forbhais Droma Dámhgháire, The Siege of Knocklong* (Cork, 1992). His doctoral thesis is on 'The Rites of Brigid-the Goddess and the Saint'.

DIARMUID Ó LAOGHAIRE has been one of Ireland's chief researchers and writers on Irish spirituality throughout the twentieth century. He lectured for many decades on Irish spiritual tradition at the Milltown Institute of Theology and Philosophy, Dublin. He has contributed numerous articles on this subject to periodicals in both Irish and English. Among the books he has also collaborated on, are *Old Ireland* (1965), *Irish Spirituality* (1981), *An Léann Eaghasta – 1000-2000* (1982), *Machnamh* (BÁC, 1992). His *Ár bPaidreacha Dúchais* (BÁC 1975) is our finest collection of traditional prayers and has been republished on four occasions. In honour of his contribution to Irish studies, Diarmuid was presented in 1997 with *Cothú an Dúchais: Aistí in Ómós don Athair Diarmuid Ó Laoghaire SJ* (BÁC 1997).

KATE FITZPATRICK is a teacher, musician and dramatherapist. She is originally from Lisburn in Northern Ireland and has a background in environmental science and in Jungian psychology. Kate spent four years on Inis Mór, Aran Islands, County Galway, exploring the mythic unconscious and its connections to landscape, Celtic myth and the Irish psyche, through shamanic work, personal healing and dance. She has trained with Paul Rebillot in the United States, in the art of using mythology, drama, gestalt therapy and ritual to create experiential healing journeys. She now lives in Inisowen, County Donegal.

JOHNSTON MCMASTER is a Methodist minister who has served Methodist congregations in West Cork, Wicklow and North Belfast. For eight years he was General Secretary of the Irish Methodist Youth Department and has worked with Youth Link, NI, the inter-church youth agency, in the development of community relations and reconciliation work. At present he is lecturer in ecumenical theology and co-ordinator of the Northern Ireland Adult Education Programme with the Irish School of Ecumenics. He has been very much involved with the development of the recent inter-church fora in Northern Ireland and is a co-ordinator of the Methodist Inter-Church Relations Committee. Publications include *Churches Working Together* and *The Future Returns; A Journey with Columba and Augustine of Canterbury*, as well as various publications on community relations issues. He leads workshops, seminars and retreats as well as teaching courses on Celtic spirituality. Regular contributions are made to BBC Radio 4, Radio 2 and Radio Ulster and a major concern is with applying faith in the public place.

DARA MOLLOY practises as a priest in the Celtic tradition. He lives on Inis Mór, Aran Islands, County Galway, where he and his wife, Tess Harper, run a spiritual centre called An Charraig. Pilgrimage groups and study groups to Inis Mór use him as a guide, and he has published a guidebook to the island entitled *Legends in the Landscape*. He is co-editor of *Aisling* magazine and has contributed to a number of other publications. He and Tess have three children.

NÓIRÍN NÍ RÍAIN is an internationally renowned spiritual singer who was born in Caherconlish, County Limerick in 1951. She studied music in University College, Cork, and graduated with a Masters degree in traditional religious song in Irish in 1980. Her vast repertoire includes a trilogy of recordings with the Benedictine monks of Glenstal Abbey: *Caoineadh na Maighdine, Good People All* and *Vox De Nube* (CD and cassette, Gael Linn). Her solo recordings include among others, *Stór Amhrán, Soundings* and *Celtic Soul*. Nóirín is author of three books, the most recent being *Gregorian Chant Experience* (Dublin: O'Brien). She has sung at four United Nations Conferences and shared performances with Gregory Peck, Anjelica Huston, Sinéad O'Connor, John Cage and His Holiness, XIV Dalai Lama. Nóirín now lives in County

Tipperary – with her husband Mícheál Ó Súilleabháin, and her two sons – where she continues to perform and write.

JOHN MORIARTY is a well-known philosopher-gardener and storyteller. A native of County Kerry, he was educated at Moyvane, Listowel, St Patrick's Training College and UCD. He taught English literature for six years at the University of Manitoba, Canada. In the mid-seventies he came back to Ireland and worked as a gardener in Connemara, County Galway. His first book, *Dreamtime* (Lilliput, 1994), was received with acclaim. It was followed by a trilogy, *Turtle Was Gone a Long Time: Vol, One Crossing the Kedron* (Lilliput, 1996), *Vol. Two, Horsehead Nebula Neighing* (Lilliput, 1997) and *Vol. Three, Anaconda Canoe* (Lilliput. 1998). Sometime lecturer and broadcaster, in 1997 John hosted a major RTÉ television series, *The Blackbird and the Bell*, which is also the title of his contribution to this collection. John is currently working on an autobiography. He lives in the Horses Glen at the foot of Mangerton Mountain near Killarney, County Kerry.

MICHAEL RODGERS is a member of St Patrick's Missionary Society, Kiltegan, County Wicklow. He lives and works in Glendalough, where he leads groups on pilgrimage through the early monastic sites. He also offers accommodation to those who want to stay for a few days retreat. He is co-author with Marcus Losack of *Glendalough; A Celtic Pilgrimage* (Dublin: Columba, 1996). **Gill MacCarthy**, who assists Michael in writing *Glendalough; A Valley of Dreams*, lives and works in County Wicklow. She has collaborated with Michael for a number of years in the development of his initiative in Glendalough. Michael may be contacted at Brockagh, Glendalough.

MARY MINEHAN is a native of Puckane, Nenagh, County Tipperary. A Brigidine Sister, she is a primary school teacher by profession and has taught in schools in Kilkenny, Laois, and Dublin. She did further studies in Mount Oliver Catechetical Centre, Dundalk, and spent five years on retreat work in schools and parishes around Ireland. In 1992, she and another sister opened a Centre for Celtic Spirituality at Solas Bríde, 14 Dara Park, Kildare Town. She is co-author of a forthcoming publication, *Rekindling the Flame – A Pilgrimage in the Footsteps of Brigid of Kildare* (Kildare, 2000).

NUALA AHERN is the Green Party MEP for Leinster. She was first elected to the European Parliament in 1994 after serving for three years on Wicklow County Council. This year (1999) she was re-elected to Europe for a second term. Nuala is a psychologist by profession and lives in Greystones, County Wicklow with her husband Barry. She is a founder member of the Irish Women's Environmental Network.

FIONNUALA NÍ CHUILL was born in Dublin and is a native speaker of Irish. A St Louis Sister, she has a BA in Celtic studies, a HDip. in education (UCD) and an MA in spirituality (Gonzaga University, Washington, USA). She is a spiritual director and a retreat facilitator. In 1984, she co-founded the Síol Retreat – a lay retreat movement – of which she is national director. She may be contacted c/o St Louis Convent, Rathmines, Dublin 6.

NOTES

THE UNCREATED CONSCIENCE OF OUR RACE

1. *Thesaurus Paleohibernicus* 2, p. 247.
2. 'Life of Columcille, Sancti Columbani Opera' in Walker, G. S. M. (ed.), *Scriptores Latini Hiberniae* 2 (Dublin, 1957).
3. Flower, Robin, *The Irish Tradition* (Dublin: Lilliput Press, 1994), pp.19-23.
4. Miles, Margaret, *Practicing Christianity* (New York: Crossroad, 1988), p. 54.
5. Cited in Ó Laoghaire, Diarmuid, 'Old Ireland and Her Spirituality', in Condren, M. (ed.), *Celtic Theology: Movement Pamphlet* No. 33 (Student Christian Movement Publications, 1977).
6. These words, found in Codex Boernerianus, were written by Sedulius. They are thought to be linked with Brigit and are partially echoed in words in the Appendix of *Bethu Brigte*. However, there they refer to Brigit's craftsman, 'Condla. Cogitosus' *VB*, however, connects the vestments with Conleth, her bishop. cf., Donncha Ó hAodha (ed.),*Bethu Brigte*, 1978, pp. 34-64 and Flower, R., op. cit., p. 39.
7. Whyte, David, 'John Scotus Eriugena' in *Celtic Theology*, op. cit., p. 13.
8. Joyce, James, *Portrait of the Artist as a Young Man* (Middlesex: Penguin, 1968), pp. 252-3.

CELTIC SPIRITUALITY: A HOLY EMBRACE OF SPIRIT AND NATURE

1. Yeats, W. B., *Vision Writings*.
2. Streit, Jakob, *Sun and Cross* (Edinburgh: Floris, 1984), p. 58.
3. Murray, Patrick (ed.), *The Deer's Cry* (Dublin: Four Courts, 1985), p. 19.
4. Ibid., p. 17.
5. Carney, James, *Medieval Irish Lyrics* (Dublin: Dolmen, 1985), p. 5.
6. Ibid., p. 7.
7. Massingham, J. H., in Bamford, Christopher and Parker-Marsh, William, op. cit., p. 7.
8. Fox, Mathew, *Meditations with Meister Eckhart* (USA: Bear & Co., 1982), p. 39.
9. Toulson, Shirley, *The Celtic Alternative* (Century, 1987), p. 66.
10. Ibid., p. 65.
11. Flower, Robin, *The Irish Tradition*, quoted in Bamford, Christopher and Parker-Marsh, William, op. cit., p. 42.
12. Carmichael, Alexander (ed.), *Carmina Gadelica – Charms of the Gaels – Hymns and Incantations,* vol. 2 (Edinburgh, 1900-1971), p. 274 (full

text). This extract from O'Donoghue, N. D., *The Mountain Behind the Mountain* (Edinburgh: T. & T. Clark Ltd., 1993), pp. 16-17.

13. 'The Sun Dance and The New Moon Of Seasons' in *Selected Verses From Carmina Gadelica* (Edinburgh: Floris, 1988).

14. Matthews, Caithlín, *Little Book of Celtic Blessings* (London: Element, 1994), p. 7.

COLM CILLE: 'A MAN FOR ALL SEASONS'

1. Anderson, A. O. and M. O. (eds and trans.), *Adomnán's Vita Columbae, Life of Columba* (Edinburgh, 1961).

2. Waddell, H., *The Wandering Scholars* (Pelican, 1954), p. 40.

3. O'Donovan, J. (ed.), *The Martyrology of Donegal. A Calendar of the Saints of Ireland* (Dublin: 1864).

4. Colm O'Reilly, Bishop of Ardagh and Clonmacnoise, speaking at Mass in the thirteenth-century Cathedral of St Mary, Iona, 1997.

5. Clancy, T. O. and Márkus, G., 'Altus Prosator' in *Iona – The Earliest Poetry of a Celtic Monastery* (Edinburgh University Press, 1995), p. 47.

BRIGIT: MUIRE NA NGAEL (MARY OF THE GAEL), THE ETERNAL FEMININE IN THE CELTIC TRADITION

1. Ó Catháin, Séamas, *The Festival of Brigit: Celtic Goddess and Holy Woman* (Dublin: DBA, 1995) and Ó Duinn, Seán, *The Rites of Brigid – the Goddess and the Saint* (PhD, Maynooth, 1998). This awaits full publication. An extract may be found in Fiannachta, P. O. (ed.), *Irisleabhar Magh Nuad* (Maynooth, 1998).

2. AFRI (Action From Ireland) is an agency concerned with Irish aid to developing countries.

3. Mac Cana, Proinsias, *Celtic Mythology* (London: Hamlyn, 1970), pp. 34-5.

4. Ó hÓgáin, Dáithí, *Myth, Legend and Romance, An Encyclopaedia Of The Irish Folk Tradition* (London: Ryan, 1990), p. 60.

5. McCone, Kim, 'Brigit in the Seventh Century: A Saint with Three Lives' in *Peritia: Journal of Early Irish Historical and Linguistic Studies*, vol. 1 (Dublin, 1982), p. 110.

6. Ó Catháin, S., op. cit., p. 58.

7. Carney, James, *The Irish Bardic Poet* (Dublin: Dolmen, 1967), p. 5.

8. O' Driscoll, R. (ed.), *The Celtic Consciousness*, Introduction, xiv (Dublin, 1982).

9. Gimbutas, Marija, *The Language of the Goddess* (London: Thames and Hudson, 1989), p. 111.

10. Gimbutas, M., op. cit., Introduction/xix.

11. Cogitosus, *Vita Brigitae* (cf. Fn. 12), Esposito, Mario, *Vita 1 S. Brigitae* (*Proceedings of Royal Irish Academy*, 1912), pp. 307-26, and Ó hAodha, Donncha (ed.), *Bethu Brigte* (Dublin, 1978).

12. Connolly, Seán and Picard, J-M., 'Cogitosus: Life of Brigit', *Journal of Royal Society of Antiquaries of Ireland* (JRSAI), vol. 117, 1987, pp. 5-27.

13. 'Cogitosus VB', Preface 4, in Connolly S. and Picard, J-M., op. cit., 1987.

14. Nic Eoin, Máirín, *B'ait Leo Bean, Gnéithe den Idé-eolaíocht Inscne i dTraidisiún Liteartha na Gaeilge* (Dublin: An Clóchomhar Tta, 1998).

15. Kelly, Fergus, *A Guide To Early Irish Law* (Dublin Institute for Advanced Studies, 1988), p. 76.

16. Ó hAodha, Donnacha (ed.) and McCone, Kim, 'Bethu Brigte' in *Peritia*, vol. 1, op. cit. (1982) and Sharpe, Richard, 'Vitae S. Brigitae: The Oldest Texts', *Peritia*, vol. 1, op. cit., 1982.

17. 'Cogitosus VB', Ch. 32, in Connolly S. and Picard, J-M, op. cit., 1987.

18. Ibid.

19. 'Cogitosus VB', Ch. 21, in Connolly S. and Picard, J-M, op. cit., 1987.

20. Ó hÓgáin, Dáithí, op. cit., pp. 334-7.

21. 'Cogitosus VB', Ch. 32, in Connolly S. and Picard, J-M, op. cit., 1987.

22. I first heard the term 'folk liturgy' used by Fr Frank Fahey, *The Celtic Furrow*, Ballintubber Abbey, County Mayo.

23. Irish Folklore Collection, IFC, 901:129.

24. Ó Catháin, Séamas, *The Festival of Brigit; Celtic Goddess and Holy Woman* (Dublin: DBA, 1995), pp. 7-9.

25. Ó Catháin, S., op. cit., pp. 10-17, 41-3.

26. Ó Súilleabháin, Seán, *Lá Fhéile Bríde* (Dublin, 1977) and in Gailey, Alan and Ó hÓgáin, Dáithí (eds), *Gold under the Furze* (Dublin, 1985). Also Danaher, Kevin, *The Year in Ireland; A Calendar* (Cork, 1972), pp. 16-31.

27. Gimbutas, M., op. cit., fig. 8-2.

28. Danaher, K., op. cit., pp. 31-3, Ó Catháin, S., op. cit., pp. 10, 13.

29. Danaher, K., op. cit., pp. 24-31, Ó Catháin, S., op. cit., pp. 10-11.

30. Ó Catháin, S., op. cit., pp. 69-70.

31. Ó Catháin, S., op. cit., p. 11 and fig. 8.

32. Heaney, Seamas, 'Crossings XXX', in *Opened Ground: Poems 1966-1996* (London: Faber, 1998), p. 376.

33. Ó Catháin, S., op. cit., pp. 53-9.

34. Mac Cana, P., op. cit., pp. 34-5.

THE BIBLE, THE DESERT AND THE CELTIC TRADITION

1. Jerome, *Vita Pauli* (P. L. 23), pp. 17-30.
2. Harbison, Peter, *Irish High Crosses* (Drogheda: Boyne Valley Honey Company, 1994).
3. Leech, Kenneth, 'The God of the Desert', in *True God: An Exploration in Spiritual Theology* (London: Sheldon Press, 1985), p. 127 ff.
4. Origen, 'An Exhortation to Martyrdom', in Rowan Greer (ed.), *Classics of Western Spirituality* (New York: Paulist Press, 1979), pp. 245ff.
5. Burton-Christie, Douglas, *The Word in The Desert: Scripture and the Quest for Holiness in Early Christian Monasticism* (Oxford University Press, 1993).
6. Meinardus, Otto, *Monks and Monasteries of the Egyptian Deserts* (Cairo, Egypt: American University in Cairo Press, 1989).
7. Plummer, Charles, 'Seven Egyptian Monks in Disert Uilag' in *Irish Litanies* (London, 1925), pp. 65, 118.
8. O'Dwyer, Peter, O. Carm., *Spirituality of the Céli Dé Reform in Ireland* (Dublin: Carmelite Press, 1977).
9. Glendalough is called 'The Monastic City'. This was the name given by the Eastern Churches to denote a monastic settlement in the wilderness. For information concerning the origins of 'Monastic Cities' see Chitty, Derwas, *The Desert A City* (Oxford: Mowbrays, 1966).
10. Stranks, C. J., *The Life and Death of St Cuthbert* (London: SPCK, 1987).
11. O'Dwyer, Peter, O. Carm., *Spirituality of the Céli Dé Reform in Ireland* (Dublin: Carmelite Press, 1977).
12. Richardson, Hilary, and Scarry, John, *An Introduction to Irish High Crosses* (Cork: Mercier Press, 1990), p. 47.
13. Stokes, Whitley (trans.), *Lives of the Saints from the Book of Lismore* (Oxford: Clarendon Press, 1890), pp. 168ff.

THE CULT OF THE DEAD IN EARLY IRISH (CELTIC) SPIRITUALITY

1. Gwynn, E., 'The Rule of Tallaght', *Hermathena*, xliv, 1927, pp. 26-7.
2. Gwynn, E. and Purton, W., 'The Monastery of Tallaght', *Proceedings of the Royal Irish Academy* (Dublin: PRIA, 1911), p. 167.
3. *Journal of the Royal Society of Antiquaries of Ireland* (JRSAI), 1871, pp. 371ff.
4. O'Dwyer, P., *Céli Dé* (Dublin, 1981), pp. 100-1.
5. Gwynn, E. and Purton, W., op. cit., p. 129.
6. *Dictionary of the Irish Language* (Dublin: Royal Irish Academy, 1983), p. 73.
7. *Proceedings of the Royal Irish Academy* (PRIA, 1973), pp. 246-9.

8. *Ériu,* 1932, pp. 103-6.
9. Fraser, J., Grosjean, S. and O' Keefe, J., *Irish Texts,* I (London, 1931), p. 44.
10. *Hallel,* Spring 1987, p. 63.
11. Horn, W., White Marshall, J. and Rourke, G., *The Forgotten Hermitage of Skellig Michael* (Oxford, 1990), p. 7.
12. Horn, W., White Marshall, J. and Rourke, G., op. cit., p. 10.
13. O'Donovan, J., *Annála Ríoghachta Éireann,* Annals of the Kingdom of Ireland, 2, 666:844 (Dublin, 1856).
14. *Béaloideas,* Journal Of the Folklore of Ireland Society, 18, 1948, pp. 148, 152.
15. Ní Bhrolcháin, M., *Maol Íosa Ó Brolcháin,* Maigh Nuad, 1986, p. 42.
16. *Béaloideas* 18, op. cit., p. 149.
17. Harbison, P., *Pilgrimage in Ireland* (London, 1991), p. 89.
18. Horn, W., White Marshall, J. and Rourke, G., op. cit., pp. 15-16.
19. Rees, A. and B., *Celtic Heritage* (London, 1976), pp. 98, 371.
20. Lady Gregory, *Cuchulain of Muirthemne* (Gerrards Cross, 1970), pp. 44-5.
21. Rees, op. cit., p. 66.
22. Markale, J., *Le Christianisme Celtique et ses Survivances Populaires* (Paris, 1983), p. 109.

CELTIC PRAYER

1. Bischoff, Bernhardt, prolific scholar in medieval studies. Works include *Manuscripts and Libraries in the Age of Charlemange* (trans.), (ed.) (Cambridge, 1994); *Carmina Burana* (Munich, 1970), among many others.
2. Plummer, Charles, *Ancient Irish Litanies* (published and translated Oxford, 1910), pp. 5, 9, 21, 31.
3. Stokes, Whitley (ed.), *Vita Tripartita Sancti Patricii* (London, 1887).
4. Hogan, Edmund, *Onomasticon Goedelicum* (Dublin, 1910).
5. Walker, G. S. M., *Sancti Columbani Opera,* p. 115.
6. Plummer, C., *Vitae Sanctorum Hiberniae II,* 119, xi.
7. Murphy, Gerard (ed.), *Early Irish Lyrics* (Oxford, 1962), p. 33.
8. Stokes, W. and Meyer, K., *Archiv für Celtische Lexicographie III,* p. 232.
9. Ó Laoghaire, Diarmuid, *Ár bPaidreacha Dúchais* (Baile Atha Cliath: FÁS, 1990), p. 6.
10. Mackey, J. P. (ed), 'Prayers and Hymns in the Vernacular', in *An Introduction To Celtic Christianity* (Edinburgh: T. & T. Clark, 1989), pp. 282-3.

11. Carney, James (ed.), *The Poems of Bláthmhac Son of Cú Brettan* (Dublin, 1964), pp. 3, 49, 51.
12. *Irisleabhar Muighne Nuadhat*, 1947, lch. 47.
13. *Archivium Hibernium*, Bol, v, p. 18.

CELTIC MYTHS IN HEALING PROCESS, A JOURNEY (WITH CÚ CHULAINN) TO THE WARRIOR OF HEART

1. Sjoo, Monica and Moore, Barbara, *The Great Cosmic Mother* (Harper Collins, 1991).
2. Rolleston, T. W., *Celtic Myths and Legends* (Senati, 1994 [reprinted]).
3. Ibid.
4. Fields, Rick, *The Code Of The Warrior* (Harper Collins, 1991).
5. Rolleston, T. W., op. cit.
6. Dunn, Joseph, *Táin Bó Cuailgne* (London, 1914), and for alternative account, cf. Thomas Kinsella (trans.), *The Táin*, from the Irish epic 'Táin Bó Cuailgne' (Dublin: Dolmen, 1966).
7. Rolleston, T. W., op. cit.
8. Ibid.
9. Ibid.
10. Ibid.
11. Ibid.
12. Ibid.

CELTIC RESOURCES FOR A PEACE PROCESS

1. Connolly, Hugh, *The Irish Penitentials* (Dublin, 1995).
2. Ó Cróinín, Dáibhí, *Early Medieval Ireland 400-1200* (New York, 1995), p. 77.

CREATIVE WORSHIP IN THE CELTIC TRADITION

1. 'Tuán' in Ó hÓgáin, Dáithí, *Myth, Legend and Romance, An Encyclopedia of the Irish Folk Tradition* (New York, 1991), p. 407.
2. 'St Patrick's Breastplate' or 'The Deer's Cry' in Murray, Patrick (ed.), Meyer, Kuno (trans.), *The Deer's Cry; A Treasury of Irish Religious Verse* (Dublin: Four Courts Press, 1986), pp. 19-21.

DIGGING FOR SOUND IN THE CELTIC TRADITION

1. Matthews, P., *Sing Me the Creation* (London: Hawthorn Press, 1994), pp. 3-4.
2. *Sean-nós* refers to a traditional form of unaccompanied singing.
3. *Déise* is an old region of Munster – modern-day County Waterford.

4. Music transcribed by Nóirín Ní Ríain from singing of Pilib Ó Laoghaire. Calligraphy by Dom. Kevin Healy OSB (d. 1991).
5. Ní Ríain, Nóirín, *Caoneadh na Maighdine* (Dublin: Gael-Linn, 1979).
6. Ó Súilleabháin, Mícheál, *Vox De Nube* (Dublin: Gael-Linn, 1989).
7. Hederman, Mark Patrick, *Vox De Nube*, op. cit.
8. Rilke, R. M., *Sonnets to Orpheus*, no. 3, in *Selected Poetry of Rainer Maria Rilke* (New York: Picador, 1981), p. 231.

THE BLACKBIRD AND THE BELL: REFLECTIONS ON THE CELTIC TRADITION

1. *Dá Chích Anann* are two mountains (known as 'the paps') overlooking Killarney. They are named in honour of the Celtic goddess Anu or D'Anu. *Luachra* was the original name of the area and it was also the name of the local Munster sept. *Cú Roí Mac Dáire* was a mythical Munster king; see Ó hÓgáin, Dáithí, *Myth, Legend and Romance; An Encyclopaedia of The Irish Folk Tradition* (London, Ryan, 1990), pp. 139-42.
2. In this region, hay is gathered into *winds*. Each wind is a large gathering of hay. A wind is often referred to as a cock of hay, elsewhere.
3. A raft of hay is a smaller amount of hay than a wind.
4. Ó Duinn, Seán, *Orthaí Cosanta sa Chráifeacht Cheilteach* (Maynooth, 1990), p. 27, Pádraig 14, 11, pp. 57-68.
5. When I say Patrick I don't just mean Patrick, but all those early Christian monks, men and women, whom he represents and who compiled the protection prayers.
6. Ó hÓgáin, Dáithí, *Myth, Legend and Romance; An Encyclopaedia Of The Irish Folk Tradition* (London: Ryan, 1990), pp. 43-5.
7. Shakespeare, William, *MacBeth* (England: Wordsworth Classics, 1992), p. 53.
8. Muirchú was a seventh-century biographer of St Patrick. Cf. Bieler, Ludwig, *The Patrician Texts in the Book of Armagh* (Dublin, 1979).
9. Dillon, Myles, *Early Irish Literature* (Chicago, 1948), pp. 40-42.
10. Murphy, Gerard (ed.), *Early Irish Lyrics* (Dublin, 1998), pp. 6-7.
11. Brontë, Emily, 'Walking Out of History' in *The Oxford Anthology of English Literature*, vol. 2 (London, 1973), p. 482.
12. Wordsworth, William, *The Oxford Anthology of English Literature*, vol. 2 (London, 1973), p. 154.
13. *Nectan* is regarded as a pseudonym for the mythical king of the Tuatha Dé Danann, Nuadhu, who had his dwelling at the source of the river Boyne. *Conaire Caomh* (handsome warrior) was mythical king of Tara. Ó hÓgáin, Dáithí, op. cit., pp. 99-100; 326-7.
14. In many Gaeltacht/Irish-speaking areas, visitors are referred to by locals

as *stráinséirí* (strangers). Those trying to learn Irish are commonly referred to as the *Lá Breá(s)*, literally: a fine day (the fine day-ers). This appellation is applied to the learner because if improperly pronounced by English speakers, it sounds like the English 'bra' (as in the article of female clothing).

15. Sayers, Peig, *Machnamh Seana-mhná*, Oifig an tSoláthair (BÁC, 1939) and *Peig – A Scéal Féin*, Cl. an Talbóidigh Tta. (BÁC, 1936).
16. Kinsella, Thomas (trans.), *Táin Bó Cuailgne* (Dublin: Oxford and Dolmen, 1969) and Ó hÓgáin, D., op. cit., pp. 131-9.
17. Ó hÓgáin, D., op. cit., pp. 224-5.

GLENDALOUGH: A VALLEY OF DREAMS
1. Heaney, S., 'St Kevin and the Blackbird' in *Opened Ground; Poems 1966-1996* (London, 1998), pp. 410-11.
2. Ó Laoghaire, D., *Ár bPaidreacha Dúchais* (Dublin: FÁS, 1990), p. 61.

KILDARE TODAY: CONTINUING THE BRIGIDINE TRADITION
1. A Norwegian poem (trans. Ragny Skarsten) from a pilgrim to Solas Bríde, 14 Dara Park, Kildare.
2. Brigit is here spelt Brigid (with a 'd'). This latter is a later form than the earlier 'Brigit'; cf. Ó hÓgáin, Dáithí, *Myth, Legend and Romance; An Encyclopaedia Of The Irish Folk Tradition* (London: Ryan, 1990), p. 60.
3. From a Thomas Davis Lecture, RTÉ, 'Selected Irish Towns in the 18th Century' by Prof. John Andrews.
4. 'The Deep Well of Brigid' by Don Mullan in *Brigidine Focus*, Journal of the Brigidine Sisters, January/February 1990.
5. Brigid, wanting to procure land for her monastery, approached the King of Leinster. After much persistence on Brigid's part, he agreed to give her as much as her cloak would cover. Miraculously, it spread over the Curragh plain!
6. 'Cogitosus VB', *JRSAI*, vol. 117 (1987), pp. 5-7.
7. Giraldus Cambrensis quoted here from Patison, J., *The Cathedral Church of St Brigid* (Kildare, 1982), pp. 8-9.
8. Luka Bloom (Barry Moore), a popular Irish singer.
9. Brophy, Fr P. J., *Nenagh Guardian*, February 1993, Tipperary.
10. From a passage in the Book of Leinster, quoted in O'Curry (*Lectures*, p. 487). It appears that the place was previously named Drumcree.
11. Traditionally St Brigid's Cross has been used as a symbol of protection against the dangers of fire, famine and disease. Through AFRI's project, the cross has become an important symbol of peace-making, protesting

the dangers of the Arms Race and the scandal of hunger in a world of plenty.

12. Des Rush, 'Tatler's Parade', *Irish Independent,* January 1993.

13. Curtayne, A., *St Brigid of Ireland* (Dublin: Browne and Nolan, 1955), p. 73.

14. Ní Ríain, Nóirín, *Gregorian Chant Experience* (Dublin: O'Brien Press, 1997), p. 161.

15. 'Lake of Beer', translated from the Old Irish by Brendan Kennelly and quoted here from Nóirín Ní Ríain's *Gregorian Chant Experience* (Dublin: O'Brien Press, 1997), pp. 162-3.

16. 'Beginners' in Levertov, Denise and Sewall, M. (eds), *Cries of the Spirit: A Celebration of Women's Spirituality* (Boston: Beacon Press, 1991), pp. 181-2.

CELTIC HOLINESS AND MODERN ECO-WARRIORS

1. Duns Scotus Eriugena in Condren, Mary (ed.), *Celtic Theology Movement Pamphlet,* no. 33 (Dublin: Student Christian Movement, 1977).

2. Danaher, Kevin, *The Year in Ireland; A Calendar* (Cork: Mercier, 1972).

THE SÍOL RETREAT: A CELTIC CELEBRATION IN AN IGNATIAN SETTING

1   Carney, James, *Medieval Irish Lyrics* (Dublin: Dolmen, 1967), pp. 3-7.

2. Flower, Robin, *The Irish Tradition* (Dublin: Lilliput Press, 1994), p. 54.

3   Ó Direáin, Máirtín, *Ó Morna agus Dánta Eile* (BAC, 1974), l, p. 236.

4. Murray, Patrick (ed. & trans.), *The Deer's Cry* (Dublin: Four Courts Press, 1986), p. 237.

5. Ibid., p. 195.

6   Ó Laoghaire, Diarmuid SJ, *Irish Spirituality* (Dublin: Gill & Son, 1956), p. 16.

7. Ibid.

8. Murray, Patrick (ed.), *The Deer's Cry* (Dublin: Four Courts Press, 1986), p. 179.

9. Ó Direáin, Máirtín, *Selected Poems – Tacar Dánta* (Kildare: Goldsmith Press, 1984), pp. 8-9.

10. Ó Laoghaire, Diarmuid SJ, *Ár bPaidreacha Dúchais* (BÁC: FÁS, 1982), l, p. 59.

11. Mac Quarrie, John, *Paths in Spirituality* (London: SCM Press, 1972), pp. 122-3.

12. Taken from traditional Irish verse, Ó Laoghaire, D., *Ár bPaidreacha Dúchais,* op. cit., p. 144.

SELECT RESOURCE LIST ON CELTIC/IRISH SPIRITUALITY

GENERAL BIBLIOGRAPHY

Allchin, A. M, *Praise Above All – Discovering the Welsh Tradition* (Cardiff, 1971).

Bhreathnach, Eibhlín, *Life and People of the Middle Ages: Ireland, England, and Europe 500 to about 1300*. Textbook for schools. (Dublin, 1976).

Bradley, Ian, *The Celtic Way* (London, 1993).

Byrne, F. J., *Irish Kings and High Kings* (Batsford, 1973).

Corkery, Daniel, *The Hidden Ireland* (Cork, 1967).

De Paor, Liam, *St Patrick's World: The Christian Culture of Ireland's Apostolic Age* (Dublin, 1993).

Doherty, Charles, *Early Medieval Ireland* (Dublin: Helicon).

Duncan, Anthony, *The Elements of Celtic Christianity* (London, 1992).

Flower, Robin, *The Irish Tradition* (Dublin, 1994).

Fox, Matthew, *Original Blessing* (USA: Bear, 1983).

Hughes, Kathleen, *The Church in Early Irish Society* (London, 1966).

——. *Early Christian Ireland: Sources* (London, 1972).

Joyce, Timothy, *Celtic Christianity: A Sacred Tradition, A Vision of Hope* (USA, 1998).

Kearney, Richard (ed.), *The Irish Mind, Exploring Intellectual Traditions* (Dublin and USA, 1985).

——. *Post Nationalist Ireland* (Routledge, 1996).

Kiberd, Declan, *Inventing Ireland: The Literature of the Modern Nation* (Great Britain, 1995).

Mackey, James P. (ed.), *An Introduction to Celtic Christianity* (Edinburgh, 1989).

Mac Quarrie, John, *Paths in Spirituality* (London, 1972).

Maher, Michael (ed.), *Irish Spirituality* (Dublin, 1981).

Martin, F.X. and T. W. Moody, *The Course of Irish History* (Cork, 1994).

Matthews, Caitlin, *The Elements of the Celtic Tradition* (Dorset, 1990).

McCone, Kim, *Pagan Past and Christian Present* (Maynooth, 1990).

O'Connor, Ulick, *Celtic Dawn* (Dublin, 1998).

O'Donoghue, Noel Dermot, *The Mountain Behind the Mountain: Aspects of the Celtic Tradition* (Edinburgh, 1993).

O'Driscoll, Robert (ed.), *The Celtic Consciousness* (USA, 1982).

O'Dwyer, Peter, *Towards a History of Irish Spirituality* (Dublin, 1995).

211

Ó hÓgáin, Dáithí, *The Sacred Isle: Belief and Religion in Pre-Christian Ireland* (Dublin, 1999).
Ó Ríordáin, John. J., *The Music of What Happens; Celtic Spirituality: A View from the Inside* (Dublin, 1996).
——. *Irish Catholic Spirituality: Celtic and Roman* (Dublin, 1998).
Ó Súilleabháin, Seán, *Irish Folk Custom and Belief* (Dublin, 1967).
Raftery, Joseph (ed.), *The Celts* (Cork, 1976).
Rees and Rees, *Celtic Heritage* (London, 1990).
Richter, Michael, *Medieval Ireland, The Enduring Tradition* (Dublin, 1988).
Ross, Anne, *Pagan Celtic Britain* (Cardinal, 1974).

APPLIED BIBLIOGRAPHY
(* indicates a key resource book)

Mythology, Folktales and Legends
*Ó hÓgáin, Dáithí, *Myth, Legend and Romance: An Encyclopaedia of Irish Folk Tradition* (London, 1990).
*Mac Cana, Proinsias, *Celtic Mythology* (London, 1970).

Campbell, Joseph, *The Hero With A Thousand Faces* (USA, 1968).
Early Irish Myths and Sagas (Penguin, 1981).
Green, Miranda Jane, *Dictionary of Celtic Myths and Legends* (London, 1992).
——. *Celtic Myths* (London, 1993).
Gregory, Lady, *Visions and Beliefs in the West of Ireland with Essays and Notes by W. B. Yeats* (London and New York, 1920).
Heaney, Marie, *Over Nine Waves* (Faber and Faber, 1994).
Kinsella, Thomas (trans.), *The Táin: From the Irish Epic Táin Bó Cuailgne* (Dublin, 1969).
MacLennan, Gordon W., *Seanchas Annie Bhán, The Lore of Annie Bhán* (ed. and trans.) A. Harrison and Máiri Elena Cook (Dublin, 1997).
Meyer, Kuno, *Cath Finntrágha* (Oxford, 1885).
——. *Aislinge Meic Conglinne* (London, 1892).
——. *The Voyage of Bran 1-2* (London, 1895-1897).
Ó Catháin, Séamas, *The Bedside Book of Irish Folklore* (Dublin, 1980).
Ó Duilearga, Séamus, *Leabhar Sheáin Í Chonaill* (Dublin, 1948), *Seán Ó Conaill's Book* (trans.) by Máire MacNeill (Dublin, 1981).
Ó hEochaidh, Seán, Ní Néill, Máire, Ó Catháin, Séamas, *Síscéalta Ó Thír Chonaill/Fairy Legends from Donegal, collected, edited, translated* (Dublin, 1977).

Ó hÓgáin, Dáithí, *The Hero in Irish Folk History* (Dublin and New York, 1985).
O'Sullivan, Seán, *Folktales of Ireland* (London, 1966)
——. *Legends from Ireland* (London, 1977).
Trevelyan, Marie, *Folklore and Folk Stories of Wales* (Elliot Stock, 1909).

Hagiography
*Kenny, James F., *The Sources for the Early History of Ireland: Ecclesiastical* (New York, 1929).

Adomnán, *Vita Columbae, Life of St Columba* (London: Penguin, 1995).
Anderson, A. O. and M. O. (ed. and trans.) *Adomnán Vita Columbae, Life of Columba* (Edinburgh, 1961).
Bieler, Ludwig, *The Patrician Texts in the Book of Armagh* (Dublin, 1979).
D'Arcy, Ryan M., *The Saints of Ireland* (Minnesota: Irish American Cultural Institute, 1985).
Forristal, Desmond, *Colum Cille: The Fox and The Dove* (Dublin, 1997).
Hanson, R. P .C., *The Life and Writings of the Historical Patrick* (New York, 1983).
Lacey, Brian, *Colum Cille and the Columban Tradition* (Dublin, 1997).
McMaster, Johnston, *The Future Returns: A Journey with Columba and Augustine of Canterbury* (Northern Ireland, 1997).
Ó hAodha, Donncha, *Bethu Brigte* (Dublin, 1978).
O'Dwyer, Peter, *Céilí Dé Spiritual Reform in Ireland 750-900* (Dublin, 1981).
Ó Fiaich, Tomás, *Columbanus in His Own Words* (Dublin: Veritas, 1974).
O'Hanlon, John, *Lives of the Irish Saints*, vols 1-9 (Dublin, 1875).
O'Meara, John. J., *The Voyage of Saint Brendan* (Dublin, 1978).
Plummer, Charles, *Vitae Sanctorum Hibernae*, 1-2 (Oxford, 1910).
——. *Bethada Náem nÉrenn* (Oxford, 1922).
Ryan, John, *Irish Monasticism* (Dublin, 1931).
Sellner, Ed, *The Wisdom of the Celtic Saints* (USA, 1993).
Stokes, Whitley, *Lives of the Saints from the Book of Lismore* (Oxford, 1890).
——. *The Calendar of Óengus* (Dublin, 1880).
Towill, E. S., *The Saints of Scotland* (Edinburgh, 1978).

Women: Mythological and Historical
Bourke, Angela, *The Burning of Brigit Cleary* (Dublin, 1999).
Chambers, Anne, *Gruanaile: The Life and Times of Grace O' Malley ca. 1530-1603* (Dublin, 1983).

Condren, Mary T., *The Serpent and the Goddess – Women, Religion and Power in Celtic Ireland* (USA, 1989 and UK, 1992).

Cosgrove, Art (ed.), *Marriage in Ireland* (Dublin, 1985).

Estés, Pinkola Clarissa, *Women Who Run With The Wolves: Myths and Stories of the Wild Woman Archetype* (London, 1992).

Gimbutas, Marija, *The Civilisation of the Goddess* (USA and London, 1991).

Green, Miranda Jane, *Celtic Goddesses: Warriors, Virgins and Mothers* (London, 1995).

Hughes, Maeve, *Epic Women: East and West – A Study with Special Reference to The Mahabarata and Gaelic Heroic Literature*, unpublished in the West, available from The Asiastic Society, 1 Park Street, Calcutta, India.

Kelly, Fergus, *A Guide to Early Irish Law* (Dublin: Institute for Advanced Studies, 1988).

Lysaght, Patricia, *The Banshee: The Irish Supernatural Death Messenger* (Dublin, 1986).

Mac Curtain, M. and Ó Corráin, D., *Women in Irish Society, The Historical Dimension* (Dublin, 1978).

Nic Eoin, Máirín, *B'ait leo Bean; gnéithe den Idé-eolaíocht Inscne i dTraidisiún Liteartha na Gaeilge* (Dundalk, 1998).

Ní Dhuibhne, Éilis, *Eating Women is Not Recommended* (Dublin, 1991).

Ó Catháin, Séamas, *The Festival of Brigit: Celtic Goddess and Holy Woman* (Dublin, 1995).

Ó Céirín, C. and K., *Women Of Ireland* (Tír Eolas, 1996).

O'Dwyer, Peter, *Mary: A History of Devotion in Ireland* (Dublin, 1988).

O'Dowd, Mary and Gialanella Valiulis, Mary Ann, *Women and Irish History* (Dublin, 1997).

Partridge, Angela, *Caoineadh na dTrí Muire* (Dublin, 1983).

Sayers, Peig, *Machnamh Seana-mhná* (BÁC, 1939), *Peig: A Scéal Féin* (BÁC, 1936) and *An Old Woman's Reflections* (trans.) Séamus Ennis (Oxford, 1972).

Celtic Calendar

*Danaher, Kevin, *The Year in Ireland: A Calendar* (Cork, 1972).

Duncan, David Ewing, *The Calendar, The 5,000 Year Struggle to Align the Clock and the Heavens – and What Happened to the Missing Ten Days* (London, 1998).

Folklore Society, England, *British Calendar Customs*, vols 1-3 (London and Glasgow, 1940).

Harrowen, Jean, *Origins of Festivals and Feasts* (London, 1980).

Mac Neill, Máire, *The Festival of Lughnasa* (Dublin, 1982).
Matthews, Caitlín, *The Celtic Book of Days* (Dublin, 1995).
Ó Catháin, Séamas, *The Festival of Brigit: Celtic Goddess and Holy Woman* (Dublin, 1995).
Santino, Jack (ed.), *Hallowe'en and Other Festivals of Death and Life* (USA, 1994).
Toulson, Shirley, *The Celtic Year* (Shaftesbury: Element, 1993).
Weiser, Francis X., *Handbook of Christian Feasts and Customs* (USA, 1952).

Pilgrimage
Pilgrimage: A Guide Book for Jubliee 2000 (Dublin: Veritas, 1998).
Harbison, Peter, *Pilgrimage in Ireland – The Monuments and the People* (London, 1991).
Haren, Michael and de Pontfarcy, Yolande, *The Medieval Pilgrimage to St Patrick's Purgatory* (Enniskillen, 1988).
Hogan, Edmund, *Onomasticon Goedelicum* (Dublin, 1910).
Joyce, P. W., *Irish Place Names* (Belfast: Appletree).
Ó Maoildhia, Dara, *Legends in the Landscape: A Pocket Guide to Pilgrimage on Árainn* (Inis Mór, Galway: Aisling Árann, 1998).
Ó Ríordáin, John. J., *A Pilgrim in Celtic Scotland* (Dublin, 1997).
Rodgers, Michael and Losack, Marcus, *Glendalough: A Celtic Pilgrimage* (Dublin: Columba, 1996).
Robinson, Tim, *Stones of Aran: Pilgrimage* (Westmeath and Dublin, 1986) and *Stones of Aran: Labyrinth* (Dublin, 1995).
Ballintubber Abbey 'Ever Ancient, Ever New', video-tape of St Patrick's Pilgrimage, *Tóchar Phádraic*, from Ballintubber Abbey to Croagh Patrick, available from Ballintubber Abbey, County Mayo.

Prayer and Reflection
*Carmichael, Alexander, *Carmina Gadelica*, 6 vols. (Edinburgh and London, 1928-71), also *Carmina Gadelica*, Complete Collection rendered into English, one vol. (Edinburgh 1992 and 1994).
*Ó Laoghaire, Diarmuid, *Ár bPaidreacha Dúchais* (Dublin, 1990).

Adam, David, *The Cry of the Deer* (London, 1987).
——. *Tides and Seasons* (London 1989).
Anderson, Rosemarie, *Celtic Oracles* (USA, 1998).
Bingen, Hildegard von, *Illuminations of Hildegard with Commentary by Matthew Fox* (USA: Bear & Co.).
De Waal, Esther, *The Celtic Way of Prayer* (London, 1996).

Dublin Diocese, *Crossing the Threshold: Jubilee 2000 Resource Book* (Dublin: Veritas).

O' Donohue, John, *Anam Chara: Spiritual Wisdom from the Celtic World* (London, 1997).

O'Driscoll, Herbert, *A Doorway in Time: Memoir of a Spiritual Journey* (New York, 1991).

Ó Duinn, Seán, *Orthaí Cosanta sa Chráifeacht Cheilteach* (Maigh Nuad, 1990).

Ó Fiannachta, P., and D. Forristal, *Saltair* (Dublin, 1988).

O' Malley, Brendan, *God At Every Grace; Prayers and Blessings for Pilgrims* (Norwich: Canterbury, 1997).

Poetry

Agnew, Úna, *The Mystical Imagination of Patrick Kavanagh; A Button Hole in Heaven* (Dublin, 1998).

Carney, James, *Medieval Irish Lyrics with The Irish Bardic Poet* (Dublin, 1990).

Heaney, Séamas, *Opened Ground Poems 1966-1996* (London, 1998).

Kavanagh, Patrick, *The Complete Poems of Patrick Kavanagh* (ed.) Peter Kavanagh (Newbridge, Ireland, 1984).

Kennelly, Brendan (ed.), *The Penguin Book of Irish Verse* (Middlesex, England, 1981).

Merriman, Brian (trans. Frank O' Connor), *The Midnight Court* (Dublin, 1989).

Murphy, Gerald, *Early Irish Lyrics* (Dublin, 1998).

Murray, Patrick (ed.) *The Deer's Cry, A Treasury of Irish Religious Verse* (Dublin, 1986).

Ní Dhomhnaill, Nuala, *Pharoah's Daughter* (Meath, Ireland, 1990).

Ó Díreáin, Máirtín, Tacar Dánta, *Selected Poems* (Kildare, Ireland, 1984).

O'Malley, Mary, *Knife in the Wave* (Ireland: Salmon, 1997).

Ó Tuama, Seán, *An Duanaire: Poems of the Dispossessed* (Portlaoise, 1991).

Yeats, W. B., *Collected Poems*, (ed.) Augustine Martin (London, 1990).

Art

Davis, Courtney, *Celtic Illumination: The Irish School* (London, 1998).

Gimbutas, Marija, *The Language of the Goddess* (USA and London, 1989).

Kelly, Eamonn P., *Early Celtic Art in Ireland* (National Museum of Ireland, 1993).

Meehan, Aidan, *Celtic Design* (London, 1991).

Meehan, Bernard, *The Book of Kells* (London, 1994).

Ó Súilleabháin, Muiris, *Megalithic Art in Ireland* (Dublin, 1993).

Richardson, Hillary and John Scarry, *An Introduction to Irish High Crosses* (Cork, 1990).

Roberts, Jack, *The Sheela-na-Gigs of Britain and Ireland: An Illustrated Guide* (Cork, 1991).

Ryan, M. (ed.), *Treasures of Ireland: Irish Art, 3000 BC-1500 AD* (Dublin, 1983).

Simms, George Otto, *Exploring The Book of Kells* (Dublin, 1989).

Zaczek, Iain, *The Art of Illumined Manuscripts* (London) and *Celtic Art and Design* (London).

JOURNALS AND PERIODICALS

Essays on Celtic spirituality and various aspects of the Celtic tradition can be found in:

* *Spirituality* (1990s), (ed.) Tom Jordan (Dublin: Domincan Publications, 42 Parnell Square), email: dompubs@iol.ie.

* *Aisling Quarterly Magazine* (1990 -), (ed.) Harper, Tess and Dara Molloy (Inis Mór, Aran Islands, County Galway, Ireland), email: aismag@iol.ie.

Béaloideas, The Journal of the Folklore of Ireland Society (Dublin, 1927 -).

Céide: Review from the Margins (Cathedral Rd, Ballina, County Mayo Ireland), email: ceide@tinet.ie.

Éigse (Dublin, 1939 -).

Ériu (Dublin, 1904 -).

Études Celtiques (Paris, 1936 -).

History Ireland: A Quarterly Magazine (History Ireland Ltd., PO Box 695, Dublin 8), email: historyireland@connect.ie.

Intercom: Pastoral and Liturgical Magazine for People in Ministry (Dublin: Veritas).

Irisleabhar Muighe Nuadhat (Maynooth, 1907 -).

Leachtaí Cholmcille (Maynooth, 1970 -).

Journal of the Royal Society of Antiquaries of Ireland (JRSAI), originally *Journal of the Kilkenny Archaeological Society* (Dublin, 1849 -).

Monastic Studies (Canada: Benedictine Priory, Montreal).

Peritia: Journal of Early Irish Historical and Linguistic Studies (Dublin, 1982 -).

Proceedings of the Royal Irish Academy (PRIA) (Dublin, 1836 -).

Sinsear (Dublin: UCD, 1979 -).

Scottish Gaelic Studies (Edinburgh, 1926 -).

Scottish Studies (Edinburgh, 1957 -).
Source Quarterly Magazine (Dublin, 1999 -).
Studia Celtica (Cardiff, 1966 -).
Studia Hibernica (Dublin, 1961 -).
The Furrow (Maynooth, Co. Kildare: St Patrick's College, 1950 -).
The Month (Middlesex, England: Jesuit Publications, Campion House).
Treoir: The Book of Traditional [Irish] Music Song and Dance (Monkstown Dublin: Comhaltas Ceoltóirí Éireann), tel. (+353-1) 2800295.
Ulster Folklife (Belfast, 1955 -).
Zeitschrift für Celtische Philogogie (ZCP) (Halle, 1896 -).

AUDIO CASSETTES AND CDs

Anúna, Vocal and Instrumental Broad Span of Irish Music (Dublin: Windmill Lane).
Arbuckle, Roy, *Lake of Shadows* (Inch Island, County Donegal, Ireland: Meitheal Publications).
Boyle, Carmel, *Celtic Songs of Earth and Heaven* (County Meath: Croí Productions).
——.*Celtic Dawn* (County Meath: Croí Productions).
Davey, Shaun, *The Pilgrim; A Celtic Suite for Orchestra, Soloists, Pipe Band and Choir* (Dublin: Tara Music).
Dublin Diocese, *Seinn Alleluia, Music for Celebrating Jubilee 2000* (Dublin: Columba, 1999).
Enya, *The Celts* (BBC Enterprises Ltd., 1990).
Lawton, Liam (ed.), *In Caelo: Songs for a Pilgrim People* (Dublin: Veritas, 1999).
——.*Light the Fire* (Dublin: Veritas).
——.*The Cloud's Veil* (Dublin: Veritas).
Mac Manus, Clement, *Compositions and Arrangements for Masses Based on the Celtic Tradition*, c/o Redemptorist Fathers, Marianella, Rathgar, Dublin 6.
Morris, Michael, *Ériu's Child* (Grattan St, Sligo: Grosvenor Productions).
Ní Mhiolláin, Treasa, *An Clochar Bán*, Sean-Nós Singing (Cló Iar-Chonnachta Teo, 1989).
Ní Ríain, Nóirín, *Caoineadh na Maighdine* (Dublin: Gael Linn).
——.*Good People All* (Dublin: Gael Linn).
——.*Vox De Nube* (Dublin: Gael Linn).
Ní hUallacháin, Gerry and Eithne, *Brigit's Kiss* (Dundalk: Lá Lugh).
Ó Riada, Seán, *Ceol an Aifrinn* (Dublin: Gael-Linn).

Comhaltas Ceolt.óirí Éireann, The National and International Association for Traditional Irish Musicians provides classes countrywide and worldwide in traditional Irish music, dance, and sean-nós singing. It also gives formal concerts, shows, sessions and exhibitions. Comhaltas has also published numerous recordings. c/o 32 Belgrave Square, Monkstown, County Dublin. Tel. (+3531) 280 0295.

RETREATS AND PILGRIM WALKS ON CELTIC SPIRITUALITY AVAILABLE FROM:

Aisling Árann An Charraig, Inis Mór, Aran Islands, County Galway Ireland), email: aismag@iol.ie.
Aran Bardic Learning. Pilgrimages and Lectures, Aran Islands, Padraigín Clancy, c/o Department of Irish Folklore, University College Dublin, email: donclancy@connect.ie, tel. (01) 269 3947.
Bard Productions. 33 Springfield Road, Terenure, Dublin 6, email: bard@bard.ie.
Céile Dé Teo. Ecumenical pilgrimages and studies on Celtic spirituality, c/o Rev. Marcus Losack, Castle Kevin, Annamoe, County Wicklow.
Celtic Furrow Retreat. c/o Ballintubber Abbey, Ballintubber, County Mayo, tel./fax: 094-30934.
Celtic Spirituality Countrywide. Broadcasting, lectures, seminars retreats, creative liturgy, pilgrim walks and tours, with Irish folklorist Padraigín Clancy, c/o Department of Irish Folklore, University College Dublin, email: donclancy@connect.ie, tel. (01) 269 3947.
Connemara College of Natural Healing. Retreats, pilgrimages, storytelling. c/o 73 Claremont Road Galway, County Galway, email: faherty@iol.ie.
Creative Courses in Fine Art and Celtic Studies. Connemara West Centre, Letterfrack, County Galway, tel. 353 (0) 95-41047.
Cultural Holidays – Celtic Spirit. c/o Elisabeth Zollinger, Inis Mór, Aran Islands, Co. Galway. (May-Oct.) and Neumarkt 11, 8001 Zúrich, Switzerland (Nov-April).
Díseart: Celtic Educational and Cultural Institute/Institiúid Oideachais agus Chultúir Ceiltigh. c/o Diarmuid Ó Dálaigh (Manager/Bainisteoir), Green Street, Dingle, County Kerry, tel. 066-915 2476.
Esker Retreat House, Athenry, County Galway.
Gate Keeper Trust: Sacred Sites and Landscape of Ireland. 154 South Park Road, Wimbledon, London SW19 8TA, England.
Glendalough: An Clochán Retreat Centre. Genevieve Mooney, Dominican Sisters, tel./fax: 0404-45137, international 353 404 45137.

Glendalough: Pilgrim Walks and Retreats. Michael Rodgers, Brockagh, Glendalough, County Wicklow.

Holy Hill Hermitage, Spiritual Life Institute, Skreen, County Sligo.

Inis Oírr, Aran Islands. Guided pilgrim walks and instruction in Irish language and traditional music. c/o Mícheál Ó hAlmhain, Inis Oírr, Aran Islands, County Galway, email: almhain@iol.ie.

Journey to the Heart and Soul of Ireland. Tours, retreats, seminars based on Celtic tradition. Details from Dolores Whelan, Education for Changing Times, Ravensdale, Dundalk, Ireland, tel./fax 042-9371901.

Lough Derg. One-day and three-day pilgrimages. c/o Parish Priest, Lough Derg, County Donegal, tel. 072-61518.

Mythic Journeys and Soul Retreats. Details from Kate Fitzpatrick, Mossy Glen, via Carndonagh, County Donegal, email: katebear@iol.ie.

Síol Retreat Centre. c/o Fionnuala Ní Chuill, St Louis High School, Rathmines, Dublin 6.

Solas Bríde. Centre for Celtic Spirituality in the Spirit of Brigit of Kildare, 14 Dara Park, Kildare, County Kildare.

Time Out. Days and weekends in Shekina sculpture garden. c/o Catherine Mac Cann, Glenmalure, County Wicklow.

Tóchar Phádraic (Croagh Patrick Pilgrimage). c/o Ballintubber Abbey, Ballintubber, County Mayo, tel./fax: (094)-30934.

Walking Ireland. c/o Michael Gibbons, Clifden, Connemara, County Galway, email: walkwest@indigo.ie.

Youth Activities. Pilgrim walks, retreats, etc. based on Celtic spirituality. Contact Catholic Youth Council, Headquarters, 20 Arran Quay, Dublin 7, tel. (01) 8725055.

There are also numerous weekend and week-long retreats available on Celtic Spirituality in many catholic retreat and pastoral centres around Ireland. For details, see The Irish Catholic Directory (Dublin: Veritas).

FULL-TIME AND PART-TIME COURSES ON CELTIC SPIRITUALITY ARE AVAILABLE IN:

Adult Education College, Sion Hill, Blackrock, County Dublin, tel. (01) 2882075.

All Hallows College, Grace Park Road, Drumcondra, Dublin 9, Ireland, tel. (01) 837 3745, email: ahallows@iol.ie (courses include annual summer school with Seán Ó Duinn and panel).

Anam Chairde Network, An Organisation Promoting the Study of Celtic Spirituality, enquiries c/o The Prior, Glastonbury Abbey, Hingham, Massachusetts, USA.

Avila Carmelite Centre of Spirituality, Morehampton Road, Donnybrook, Dublin 4, Ireland, tel. (01) 668 3155.

Díseart: Celtic Educational and Cultural Institute/Institiúid Oideachais agus Chultúir Ceiltigh (Popular Courses and Diploma/Degree courses offered in Irish and English with accreditation under Maynooth Pontifical University from 2000), c/o Diarmuid Ó Dálaigh, Manager/Bainisteoir, Green Street, Dingle, County Kerry, tel. 066-9152476.

Dowdstown House, Dalgan Park, Navan, County Meath, Ireland, tel. 046-21407.

Institute For Feminism and Religion, Unit 8, Terenure Enterprise Centre, 17 Rathfarnham Road, Dublin 6W, Ireland, tel./fax 3531 4901917, website: http://www.anu.ie/ifr (courses offered in Irish women's wisdom, Celtic heritage, theology, philosophy, feminist studies and the creative arts, also, celebration of Celtic festivals and publications), Director: Mary Condren ThD.

Irish School of Ecumenics. Ecumenical Studies and Centre for Peace Studies, Development Office, Bea House, Milltown Park, Dublin 6, Ireland, tel. (01) 260 1144.

Lampeter University: Undergraduate and Postgraduate Courses available in Celtic Christianity, Lampeter, Wales, United Kingdom.

Mater Dei Institute of Education, Clonliffe, Dublin 3, Ireland, tel. (01) 837 6027.

Mary Immaculate College, Limerick City, Ireland, tel. 061-313632.

Milltown Institute of Theology and Philosophy, Milltown Park, Sandford Road, Dublin 6, Ireland, tel. (01) 269 8388 and fax (01) 269 2528.

There are also full-time and part-time degree and diploma courses available in Celtic studies at most third-level universities, colleges and institutions in Ireland. (While excellent and useful, these courses tend not to focus on spirituality or prayer).